BRIDGES!

AMAZING STRUCTURES TO DESIGN, BUILD & TEST

Carol A. Johmann and
Elizabeth J. Rieth

Illustrations by
Michael Kline

A WILLIAMSON *KALEIDOSCOPE KIDS*™ BOOK

DEDICATION

To all those who have a dream and dare to build it.
And to our young bridge builders —
Christine and David Rieth, Stephen Burke,
and Kate and Alex Brett.

ACKNOWLEDGEMENTS

Many thanks to Gabriel Del Vecchio, P.E.,
Chris Bollin, Louis Chrzasc, and Tom Lehmkuhl, P.E.
for their valuable information and advice,
and to John Rieth for all his help and encouragement.

Library of Congress Cataloging-in-Publication Data

Johmann, Carol, 1949-
   Bridges!: amazing structures to design, build & test / Carol Johmann
   & Elizabeth Rieth; illustrations by Michael Kline.
      p.   cm.
   "A Williamson Kaleidoscope Kids book"
   Summary: Describes different kinds of bridges, their history, dilemmas, safety,
and more.
     ISBN 1-885593-30-9 (alk. paper)
     1. Bridges—Juvenile literature. [1. Bridges.] I. Rieth, Elizabeth, 1957-
II. Kline, Michael P., ill. III. Title.
TG145.J57   1999
624'.2—dc21   98-53272
                CIP

JNF
624.2
Johmann
96 p.: ill.
Includes index

Photographs: **Boily**, page 50; **Charles M. Hiller/Golden Gate Bridge, Highway and Transportation District**, page 66; **Courtesy of the Frances Loeb Library, Graduate School of Design, Harvard University**, page 70; **Library of Congress, Prints and Photographs Division, Detroit Publishing Company Collection**, page 35; **Library of Congress, Prints and Photographs Division, HAER**, page 44 (NY,1-ALB,19-11), page 56 (NY,31-NEYO,90-;DLC/P14/Jet Lowe), page 66 (CAL,38-SANFRA,140-20), page 85 (NH,10-CORN,2-); **Mansell/TIME, Inc.**, page 48; **National Park Services**, page 24; **Roebling Collection. Archives and Special Collections, Rensselaer Polytechnic Institute, Troy, NY**, page 59; **T.Y. Lin**, page 88; **Underwood Photo Archive, S.F.**, page 47; **University of Washington Libraries, Special Collections**, page 64 (Neg.#Farqharson 4, 6, 12)

Kaleidoscope Kids™ Series Editor: **Susan Williamson**
Design: **Joseph Lee Design: Danny Yee, Sue Yee, Joseph Lee**
Illustrations: **Michael Kline Illustration**
Printing: **Quebecor Printing, Inc.**

Printed in Canada

Williamson Publishing Co
P.O. Box 185
Charlotte, Vermont 05445
1-800-234-8791

10 9 8 7 6 5 4 3 2 1

Contents

Take the CHALLENGE!

Would you like to be a bridge builder? It won't be easy. You'll need to be part scientist, part architect, part environmentalist, part innovator, and part historian. And, oh, the decisions you'll have to make! Should you build a graceful arch, a sturdy beam, or a soaring suspension bridge over that rushing river? How will you put up piers in the middle of the water? What materials should you use — concrete, steel, or wood? And what types of workers will you need? Every decision you make will be important. One mistake and your bridge could come tumbling down! And, yes, that has happened more than once!

The story of bridges is the story of people who have a dream and struggle to make it come true. It is the story of how beauty and strength combine in structures that help us connect our lives with each other across expanses of water and land.

It's an old story, starting long ago, but it's a new story, too. Today's steel and concrete bridges soar to incredible heights and lengths. They don't look at all like simple bridges of long ago. Or do they? If you look closely, all the parts are the same. The reasons they stand are the same. The forces at work are the same. In fact, even the designs are the same. Since ancient times, people have used three basic bridge designs to cross the rivers and gorges in their way: the arch, the beam, and the suspension.

So, come explore the fascinating world of bridges. Be a full participant, take challenges, build bridges, and test loads. Let your inventive mind and spirit spark new ideas that could help bridge our world — today to tomorrow!

Engineer Mason Environmentalist

WHAT DO YOU WANT TO BE?

As with just about everything else, people make them happen. Bridges, that is. Bridges (except for the rare natural bridge) are made by people like you. Men and women work in areas of planning and construction that use their individual skills and talents. Although they specialize in one area — say, pouring the foundation in deep water — they need to understand the whole process.

So as you build the bridges in this book, consider what aspects most interest you and suit your individual talents.

BE A BRIDGE BUILDER

Investigate bridge designs, the forces that act on bridges, and the materials that stand up to those forces. It's all right here! And, every so often, you will be asked to be a bridge builder. You'll be the one who has to choose among arch, beam, and suspension designs. You'll have to figure out what materials to use. There'll be lots of decisions to make and problems to solve.

PICTURE YOURSELF!

- Would you rather be the *bridge designer* (determining how it will look), *engineer* (figuring loads and materials), *supervisor* (organizing work crews), or *construction worker*?

- Are you a *creative problem solver*? Then, maybe you can figure out how a bridge will be built in raging water or across a massive canyon.

- Are you good at *budgeting money*? Where will the money come from to pay the workers and buy materials?

- Are you an *environmentalist* who is willing to fight to preserve the natural order of the world? What will the bridge do to the environment and to the communities it joins?

- Are you good at *organizing people*? Then, maybe you would enjoy being a shift supervisor.

- Do you like good hard work where your body and mind must be focused in tough conditions? Perhaps you want to be one of the actual *construction workers*.

- Do you have a good *sense of design and function*? Then, perhaps you can make the decisions about what kind of bridge to build to best suit the site, the budget, and the use of the bridge.

Every person involved in planning and building a bridge is essential to the total project, and the more talented and dedicated each is, the more likely the bridge will be a success.

How the Romans Did It

The ancient Romans were amazingly organized. After all, when you build a great and powerful empire, many cities, roads, and bridges must be built, too. To get everything done, the Romans ranked each person in the empire — from the most knowledgeable engineer to the hardworking slaves — into a pyramid of power called a *hierarchy*.

Slaves and workers were at the bottom of the Roman hierarchy. The people with skills, like engineers, carpenters, surveyors, and masons, were above them. Above the skilled people were government officials who oversaw the project. At the top of it all was the Emperor, who approved all major works of construction.

Think About It

Division of Labor

One way to think about the pyramid-shaped hierarchy is to picture yourself somewhere on it. Imagine being the mason as compared with the government officials. And what would your life be like as the slave at the bottom of the pyramid?

Picture a hierarchy today. How do you think people are treated and paid at various points on the hierarchy? Sketch a picture of your school hierarchy. Where do you think the students fit? Can you come up with other shapes — like a wheel or a chain — that might work differently?

BRIDGE BUILDING:
THE PLANNING PHASE

Surveyors and **mapping experts** measure the size of the available land and how high or low the ground is to see if a bridge will fit. They make special maps that show what the area looks like.

The **architect** helps the designer make sure the bridge will look good in its surroundings.

The **bridge designer** is in charge of the whole project but depends on many experts to help. Before planning and designing a bridge, the designer needs to know everything about the bridge and the site where it's to be built.

1, 2, or 3 lanes?

The **planning expert** has the very first job in building a bridge. It's his or her job to see if a bridge really has to be built and how big the bridge has to be.

The **soils engineer** drills deep holes into the ground and then takes soil and rock samples from these holes. The samples tell whether the ground is strong enough to hold up a bridge, where the foundations of the bridge should go, and how deep the foundations need to be.

Who Does What?

The **aerial photographer** takes pictures of the site from an airplane before the bridge is built. These photographs help the surveyors do their job.

CLICK!

The **traffic and safety expert** learns about the car accidents that have happened at the site in the past to help the designer plan a bridge that will make travel safer.

TRAFFIC REPORTS

The **landscape architect** and **environmentalist** make sure the bridge won't disturb wetlands and wildlife areas or cause other problems. They also figure out where to place trees and other plants after the bridge is built, and where to put in bike paths and walkways.

continued

Visit a Construction Site

Seeing is believing, that's for certain! And there is nothing more exciting than seeing the stages of building a bridge.

You'll want to make your visit before the bridge building begins, if possible, and then at regular intervals as it goes up. See if the person in charge (the foreman) or one of the engineers will show you the site and explain why the bridge is being built where it is. What is the ground like underneath?

Ask lots of questions so you, the foreman, and the future bridge can become good friends!

Learn the Lingo

Staking out is surveyors' talk for figuring out where and how deep the bridge's supports have to be.

THE BUILDING PHASE

The **bridge designer**, sometimes with the help of a **structural engineer**, approves the design. The designer finds a contractor to build the bridge. The contractor who offers the lowest bid, or price, to build the bridge safely usually wins the contract.

The **inspector** visits the bridge site and checks the work of the contractor and workers, reporting back to the designer about any problems.

The **project superintendent** is assigned by the contractor to hire the workers, order the materials, get equipment to the site, and schedule the work.

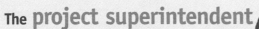

The **contractor** is in charge of building the bridge, working with the bridge designer and inspector to make the plan a reality.

The **foremen** (both men and women are called foremen) help the project superintendent with specific jobs. One is in charge of all the stone and cement workers, or masons, on the bridge; another is in charge of the carpenters; another, the steel workers; and so on.

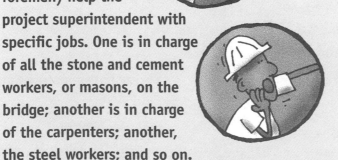

The **builders** include the cement masons, steelworkers, carpenters, truck drivers, equipment operators, electricians, and other construction workers who actually build the bridge.

Organize a Kitchen Cleanup

Design a team structure of your family to organize cleaning up after dinner. Is it a pyramid or wheel design? Choose a supervisor and the skilled workers. Then, when the last dish is put away, discuss how things went. Was everyone happy with his or her job? Are there ways you could improve the system? Take turns being the supervisor throughout the week. Which job do you like best?

Teamwork!

No doubt about it! There's a real art to being a team player. You have to know how to cooperate and that means you have to be willing to compromise. In today's workplace, almost everything is done in teams: team teaching, team advertising campaigns, sports teams, and rock bands.

Have you ever been on a team? What could you do to help your team work better? And what do you do if someone not only doesn't help the team, but causes problems so no one can get anything done?

Bridge building takes a tremendous amount of teamwork. If you were in charge of making the whole project work, what would you do to keep the teams working well together?

Bridge-Building BASICS

Y ou and your friends are hiking through the woods when you come upon a stream. Someone's put a plank of wood across it, and you walk across. But instead of holding you up, it sags and dips into the water. The next thing you know — splash! — your feet are all wet. Some bridge! That plank bridge held up its own weight, but it couldn't support yours. What could you do to make it work better?

Push & Pull

The way a bridge works is a lot like playing tug-of-war when there is no winner. If both sides are weighted equally, the rope and all the players balance and stay put. That's what a good bridge does. But if one side is stronger, down comes the other! (Uh-oh! That's when bridges "all fall down"!)

The goal in these games is to stay put and not tug the other side off balance. Ask at least three friends to join you; then, choose sides so each team is about equal in strength.

A bridge's job is to support its own weight and the weight of all the traffic that crosses it. Bridge builders call the weight of the bridge itself *dead load*, because once the bridge is built, the dead load stays the same. Guess what they call the weight of the traffic? Yes, *live load* is right! The live load changes all the time.

Be a suspension bridge cable

Line up side by side, with everyone holding hands. Start pulling apart at the center, but don't pull so hard that players fall down. Remember, you want to stay up, so if one team is stronger, the players on that team have to pull less. As you pull, feel the tension (stretch) *in your arms and shoulders. Now you know what it's like to be a cable on a suspension bridge.*

continued

Be a stone in an arch bridge

The players on each team line up, one behind the other, facing the other team. The middle two players place their hands on each other's shoulders. The outside players put their hands on the waist of their teammate in front of them. Once you're set, start pushing. Again, push equally so everyone stays up. As you're pushed, feel the compression (pushing) *force that squeezes your body. That's what it's like to be a stone in an arch or a support under any bridge.*

Balance like a bridge

Now try pulling and pushing. Line up side by side with some space in between. The two in the middle lean towards each other so their shoulders touch. They also hold hands with the players on the outside. All other outside players also hold hands. While the middle two push against each other, the outside players pull. Can you push and pull so everyone stays put? Who feels both compression and tension?

A BALANCING ACT

For a bridge to stand, it must support its own weight. All the forces acting on it must be in balance or the bridge will fall. See for yourself how things at rest are always in balance by putting a book on a table. It's at rest, because *gravity* (the force that pulls objects toward the center of the earth) pulls down on it as much as the table pushes up on it.

Now, give the book a push or pull. To move it, you had to apply a force, right? But if you push it equally in opposite directions, what happens? Yup, the forces are in balance and the book won't move. The same thing happens if you pull it equally in opposite directions, or if you push and pull from the same end.

Anatomy of a Finger— er— Bridge!

Bend your finger. See how the skin on the inside of the curve gets squeezed, while the skin on the outside is stretched? Remember how the plank sagged when you walked on it? Your weight caused the wood along the top to be squeezed, or compressed, and the wood along the bottom to be stretched, or tensed. The top was compressed and the bottom was tensed — just like your bent finger, upside down.

Learn the Lingo

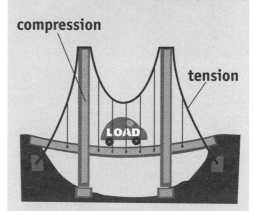

compression

tension

LOAD

May the FORCE Be With You!

Load creates two major forces that act on the parts of a bridge. One force, called *compression*, pushes on, or squeezes, bridge parts. The other force, called *tension*, pulls on, or stretches, them. For a bridge to do its work, each part of the bridge must stand up to all the pushes and pulls that act on it every day.

Wheee...

The Long & Short of It

A good way to tell whether something is being pushed or pulled is to see what happens to its length. Draw a few straight lines, about 1 inch (2.5 cm) apart, along one long edge of a slightly damp sponge. Bend the sponge into a U-shape as if a load were on it. See how the lines get closer together on the inside of the U? That's because compression makes things shorter. *On the outside of the U, the lines get farther apart.* Tension makes things longer.

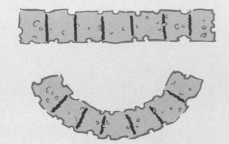

IF YOU CAN'T SEE IT, IS IT THERE?

Did you think of a way to make that imaginary plank bridge in the woods work better? Let's say you did: It works so well it no longer sags at all when you walk on it. Now think about this riddle:

**If you can't see a bridge sag
when a load is on it,
are the forces still there?**

Try This! *When you sit in a soft armchair, what happens to the cushion? Your weight pushes on it, and it compresses, or gets thinner. Now sit on a wooden chair or bench. Does the seat get thinner or the legs get shorter? Your weight didn't change, of course. You didn't push down harder on the armchair than you did on the wooden chair. So why the difference? Well, because the cushion is soft, you can see it being compressed. Because the wooden chair is hard, you can't see it happen.*

Learn the Lingo

What Makes a Bridge, a Bridge?

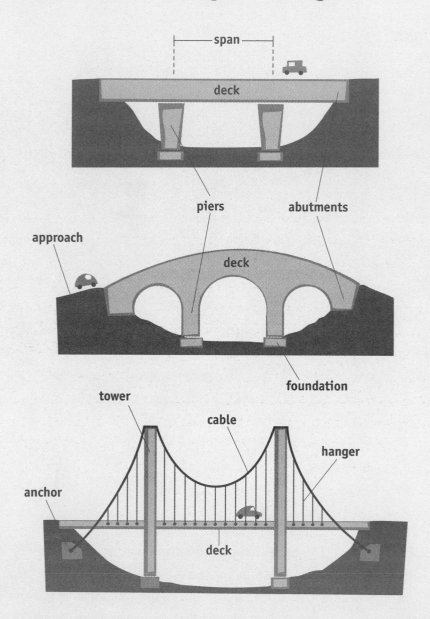

span

deck

piers

abutments

approach

deck

foundation

tower

cable

hanger

anchor

deck

If you were to travel around the world, you'd see many, many different kinds of bridges, both old and new. Bridges today may look different than bridges built long ago, but their parts are similar.

Every bridge has a *deck*, where you walk or drive. Every bridge has *supports*, too. The distance between a bridge's supports is called its *span*. All supports rest on *foundations* in the ground. And the *approaches* are the roads leading up to a bridge.

In beam and arch bridges, supports at the ends are called *abutments* and supports in the middle are called *piers*.

In a suspension bridge, the middle supports are called *towers*. Long wire *cables* are strung over the towers and secured in *anchors* on land. *Hangers* run from the cables to the deck to hold it up.

Pushes and Pulls
in Different Bridges

The basic difference between these bridge designs is how each bridge carries the weight, or load, of the bridge itself and traffic, too (see page 13).

Beam

Think about your finger again. In a beam design, the weight of the load is passed along the beam, down through the bridge supports into the ground. As the beam sags under the load, the top side of the beam is squeezed, or compressed, while the bottom side is stretched in tension.

Arch

The arch changes the downward force of gravity into a sideways push. The weight is carried along the curve to the abutments (the supports at the ends that rest on the banks) and into the ground. This creates lots of compression, but little tension.

Hidden Secrets

Remember, if a bridge is to stand, the forces acting on it must be in *balance*, which means *the forces must be opposite and equal.*

But wait! The arrows showing the pushing and pulling in each of the three bridges are not opposite each other. So how do these bridges stay in balance?

Here's a hint. The forces shown by the arrows are the pushes and pulls created by the load. The balancing forces that are opposite and equal are not shown. So what provides them? It's the same thing that pulls and pushes on you. That's right, it's the earth!

Suspension

OK, this will seem complicated, but once you get it — it's as clear as can be! The load pulls down on the hangers, which pull on the cables. The cables pull on the towers and anchors, and the anchors pull back, or *resist* the pull on them, because they're heavy and buried in the ground. All these parts are in tension. The towers are also compressed as the cables push down on them and their foundations.

Pile It On

Shapes are also important in building strong bridges. Test it out on these varied paper shapes.

Materials:

- 5 pairs of thick hardcover books for supports (The books in each pair must be the same height.)
- Stack of paper
- Paper clips, pennies, toy cars, or small blocks to use as load
- Ruler, glue, and scissors

1. *Clear off the kitchen table, because you'll need lots of space.*

2. *Stand the pairs of books upright like book-ends, each about 6 inches (15 cm) apart. Place a piece of paper across the first pair.*

3. *Curve a piece of paper upward and tuck its ends inside the book covers of another pair of books.*

4. *Gently add paper clips, one by one, to the middle of each bridge. Which one can take more load before it begins to sag?*

Now, see if the two shapes together would make a stronger bridge.

1. Glue two or three pieces of paper together end to end to make one long piece. It needs to be as high as the books are when it's propped up between them in an arch.

2. Rest a piece of paper on top. Can this bridge hold more paper clips than the first two?

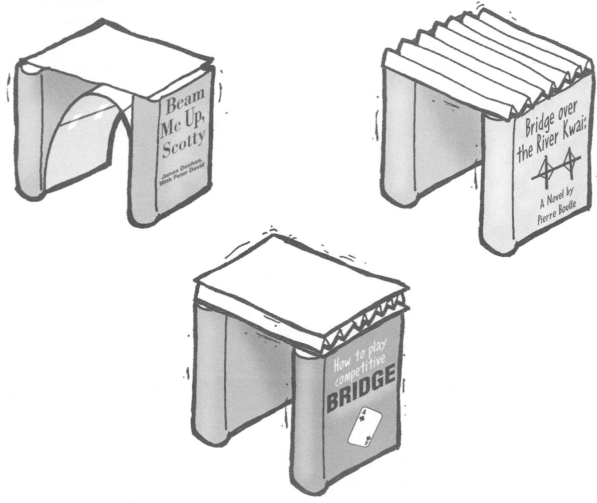

Next, try this:

1. Accordion-fold a piece of paper lengthwise. Place it across the top of the fourth pair of books.

2. Fold another piece of paper in the same way. Glue pieces of paper to its bottom and top. Try not to squish the folds. Make a fifth bridge with it.

3. Which of the last three bridges do you think is strongest? Test your guess by gradually adding load to one of them until it falls. See if the other two can carry the same or more load. Did you guess right? What could you do to make the strongest bridge even stronger?

A Bridge Builder's Checklist

The thing about bridges is that each one starts in the same way — as someone's idea. And each bridge has the same general purpose — to solve the problem of getting from here to there. Yet each bridge is different from all others, because each site presents its own challenges.

Before designing a specific bridge, engineers examine the site, looking at it from every angle. From the top of the banks to the bottom of the river, from the traffic on land to the traffic on water, they have to ask all sorts of questions.

SITE CONSIDERATIONS
- Is this bridge over water or land?
- If it's over water, how deep is it?
- How high are the banks? Are they rocky or soft?

PEOPLE/ENVIRONMENT ISSUES
- Is the waterway busy? Do tall ships pass through?
- What's the weather like? Is it very windy? Very cold? Very hot?
- Do earthquakes happen here?
- How will the bridge affect the land and wildlife in the area?
- Are there valuable fossil beds at the site?

STRUCTURAL ISSUES
- Is the bridge for trains or cars? Will pedestrians and bicyclists use it?
- How wide is the gap?
- Can the gap be crossed with a single span?
- Which kind of bridge will work best?
- What materials are available?

ECONOMIC (MONEY) ISSUES
- How much money can be spent on the project?
- Will some bridges be out of the question because they're too expensive to build?

Triumphal Arch • Paris

The Amazing
ARCH

You see them everywhere! Windows — old and new — are shaped like arches; walkways are trellised with arches covered in flowers; gates and entrances are shaped like arches. Why? Because arches are considered to be one of the most beautiful shapes in construction and are certainly one of the strongest.

When the arch was first introduced in ancient times, it was a great leap forward. Beforehand, there were mostly beam bridges with vertical wood or stone supports called *piers*. But building piers could be difficult, and they could interfere with ship traffic under a bridge. The arch bridge solved this problem, because it could be built higher than a beam bridge, allowing tall boats to pass underneath. Now that was progress!

St. Louis Arch • St. Louis, Missouri

Let a Rainbow Be Your Teacher

HOW IT WORKS!

An arch's beauty comes from its graceful curve. Its strength comes from how this curve carries weight (load) outward in both directions to the abutments at its ends.

Since everything is pushing and being pushed at the same time, all the parts of an arch are compressed (squeezed).

Stone is super strong when it's compressed, but it's weak when it's pulled, or under tension. So ancient builders figured they could span longer distances using stone arches instead of stone beams (which are both pushed and pulled). What a great observation those early builders made!

How do you think ancient peoples may have gotten the idea for curved arches? Perhaps from seeing the shape in nature — a rainbow, the entrance to a cave, or a natural rock formation like the *Rainbow Bridge* in southeastern Utah. It took millions of years for moving water to carve this arch out of pink sandstone. The Navajo people call it *Nonnezoshe,* which means "the rainbow turned to stone."

Look closely at the Rainbow Bridge, noticing how its ends are thicker than the top, like a man-made arch. (Or is it that the man-made arch is just like nature's?)

Try this! *Make the Rainbow Bridge out of clay. When it's completed, place it on its side, and cut it into wedge-shaped pieces. Can you put the pieces back together again?*

Rainbow Bridge • Utah

Build an Arch, Roman-Style

The Romans, who ruled over much of Europe for 500 years (first century B.C. to fourth century A.D.), were the first great arch bridge builders. The basic Roman arch is built starting at the abutments *(see page 17). Stones are added to both sides, higher and higher along the curve, until only one more stone, called the* keystone, *is needed at the top.*

The Romans realized long ago that it's impossible to make an arch without supporting it as it goes up. They used a wooden frame, called the centering, *to support arches as they were being built. The centering was removed after the keystone was placed.*

To build a Roman-style stone arch, you'll need some clay, Play-Doh, or homemade mortar (see page 26) *and a bunch of same-sized rocks.*

Use something as the centering for your stone and clay bridge. Perhaps you have a block that's the right shape. Or try cutting up a cylindrical container (a rounded oatmeal container works well) to get a curved surface. Then, using the clay as cement, fit the rocks together over the centering to form your arch.

Building Strength from Weakness

The famous Italian artist Leonardo da Vinci once said, "An arch consists of two weaknesses which, leaning on each other, become a strength." What a wonderful image! The two weaknesses are the arch's two halves, but when leaned against each other at the top stone, or keystone, they become strong by the force of compression. Only then can the arch support itself.

What do you think Leonardo da Vinci's observation means when applied to life in general?

Making Concrete

NOTE: *Be sure to ask for grown-up help when boiling water and cooking on the stove.*

Real mortar and concrete harden, or set, because of a chemical reaction between water and the minerals in the cement. Your home-made concrete will set because of a reaction between water and cornstarch (your cement) that creates a thick, sticky substance. Before it hardens, you'll be able to mold it into any shape.

Materials:

- Tea kettle, mixing spoon, and spatula
- Double boiler (a small pot placed inside a larger pot works well)
- 1 cup (250 ml) sand
- ½ cup (125 ml) cornstarch
- Centering frame (see page 25)
- Cookie sheet
- Handful of pebbles or gravel

1. *Boil some water in the kettle and in the bottom (larger) pot of the double boiler (with grown-up help). Meanwhile, mix the sand and cornstarch in the top (smaller) pot of the double boiler (away from the stove).*

2. *When both kettle and bottom pot are boiling, ask your helper to add ¹/₂ cup (125 ml) of the kettle's boiling water to the mixture in the top of the double boiler. Place the pot on the bottom of the double boiler. Stir as the mixture cooks. Stop when it gets thick. (If it gets too thick, add a bit more hot water.) Let it cool until you can touch it.*

Cement from a Volcano?

What's so special about *pozzolana*? The Romans made this cement with ash that was blown out of the volcano Vesuvius. The Romans dug up the ash in a town called Pozzuoli (thus its name). The magical thing about pozzolana is that it's waterproof. It hardens even when it's wet! Imagine what that meant to the Romans when it came time to build piers in water!

3. *At this stage you've made mortar. (Try using some of it to build a stone arch like the one on page 25).*

4. *Mix the pebbles into the rest of the mortar to turn it into concrete. Shape it into two piers and two thin rectangular beams. Curve one beam into a semicircular arch (see page 28).*

continued

5. *Put everything on the cookie sheet and place it in the oven at 275°F (135°C) until the objects dry.*

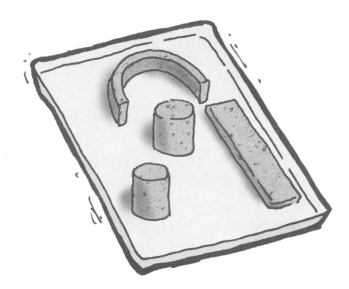

oncrete is made by mixing sand and small stones with water and cement. The cement and water form a paste that glues the sand and stones together. After sitting for a while, the mixture hardens into concrete. Like stone, concrete is strong when it's squeezed or compressed, which makes it perfect for bridge foundations and piers.

Round 'n' Round

Ever wonder why concrete trucks are always turning? It's to keep the concrete from hardening too soon. As long as the mixture is turned, it'll stay liquid until it can be poured in the right spot.

Once it has dried and cooled, examine what you've made. Does the concrete look real?

Make a beam bridge with the piers and straight beam. To compare the strength of the beam bridge to the arch, gradually add some weight to both structures by gently pressing down on both with your thumbs. Which structure cracks first under a load? Finally, see if your concrete is waterproof by putting one of the piers in water.

Build a Cofferdam

Even with waterproof concrete, you can imagine Roman engineers scratching their heads and wondering, "How are we going to pour it underwater on the bottom of a river to make foundations for our piers?" The answer they came up with is — you don't! You get rid of the water instead. That's the idea behind another of their inventions, the *cofferdam*, a round or square dam that keeps water out.

Materials:

- Pan
- Sand or dirt
- Water
- Popsicle sticks (at least 30)
- Tape
- Plastic wrap
- Turkey baster (or eyedropper)

1. *Fill the pan halfway with sand or dirt. Add water to about an inch (2.5 cm) above that.*

2. *Use a third of the Popsicle sticks to make the inside ring of the dam. Push each stick through the sand to the bottom of the pan. The sticks should touch each other and be higher than the water.*

3. *Run a piece of tape along the top of the ring on the inside. Put a second ring around the first using the rest of the Popsicle sticks, leaving about a $\frac{1}{2}$-inch (1-cm) space in between. Tape along the outside of the second ring.*

continued

4. *Twist a piece of plastic wrap and snake it around the space, stuffing it down as you go until you fill the space higher than the water. Fix the sticks if they moved.*

5. *Remove the water inside the inner ring with the baster. Can you get the inside dry? Can you at least get the water level inside lower than the water outside? If you can, you've done an excellent job! Even those master builders, the Romans, couldn't get their cofferdams completely dry!*

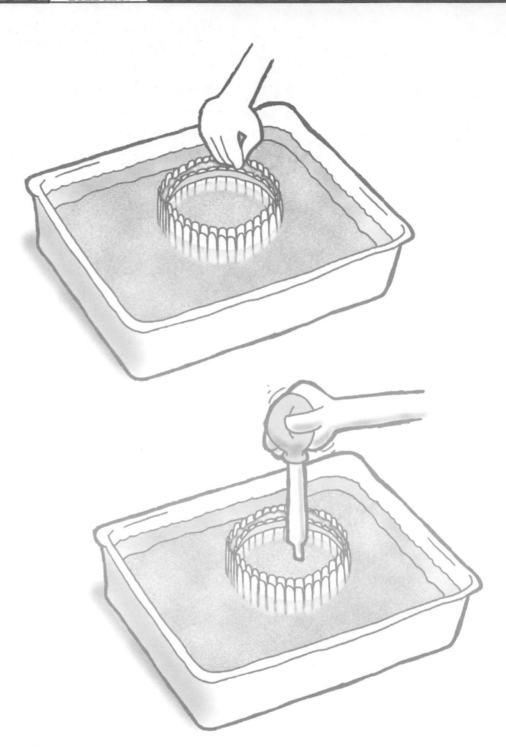

Tunneling Under

Building a tunnel that carries traffic under a river presents the same problem as putting foundations of a bridge in a river. How do you build under water? Think of ways you could change a cofferdam to build a tunnel. Remember that a cofferdam stands straight up. A tunnel lies sideways and often has to be very long. Also remember that you need to use materials that work well under water.

Working Underwater

The Romans built their coffer-dams very much the same way you just did. They drove long wooden stakes into the riverbed in two rings, one outside the other, around the site for a pier. They stuffed clay in between the rings to make the cofferdam water-tight. Workers then emptied it bucket by bucket.

Once the cofferdam was empty, pozzolana was poured in to make a foundation. Then masons laid stones on top to build the pier.

After everything set, workers removed the stakes.

Building a cofferdam like the Romans did isn't easy. Today, huge steel boxes are used instead of wooden stakes, and water is sucked up by motor-powered pumps instead of by hand. Machines *dredge*, or scoop up, mud and gravel at the bottom of the cofferdam, all the way down to the *bedrock* (the solid rock beneath the soil). Then a deep layer of waterproof concrete is poured in.

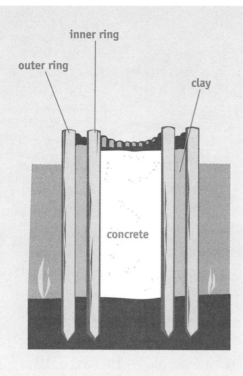

outer ring

inner ring

clay

concrete

 **PEOPLE** MAKE IT HAPPEN

A Strong Match

Joseph Monier was a French inventor who liked puttering in his garden. Once, while molding wet concrete into flowerpots, he decided to try strengthening the concrete by putting steel wires in it. His idea worked, and he made pots that were stronger and less likely to crack. He patented his new

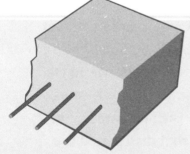

material in 1856 and went on to use it to make parts for buildings. Concrete strengthened by steel is called *reinforced concrete*. Most of the bridges you see built today are made with steel and reinforced concrete, such as the *Natchez Trace Parkway Arches* near Nashville, Tennessee.

 Learn the Lingo

Reinforced concrete is often made with steel bars, known as *rebar* (short for "reinforced bar").

Hmph! That's some flowerpot!

PEOPLE
MAKE IT HAPPEN

An Ancient Great

The *semicircular* (half-circle) *arch* met all the Romans' needs, and it met the needs of the early Chinese, too — that is, until master bridge builder **Li Chun** had to build a stone bridge over the Xiao (SHOUW) River in 600 A.D.

Li Chun couldn't build a bridge like the ones he'd built before, because the river was too wide. A single semicircular arch would have to rise very high to span the Xiao. It would be so tall and heavy, it might push the abutments apart. He couldn't build a bridge made of two arches either, because the river flowed too fast to build a pier in the middle, even with a cofferdam. And if he built a beam bridge, boats wouldn't fit

under it. A real dilemma!

But Li Chun saw a solution — a *shallow arch* that was less than half a circle. An arch like that could be made longer without getting so tall. But even a shallow-arch bridge would be so heavy it might move the abutments. So Li Chun put holes in the sides of his bridge to make it lighter. Not any old holes, though. Each hole was itself an arch that distributed the squeezing force and kept the bridge strong. Now that is a creative, inventive mind at work!

Li Chun's bridge is known as the *Anji Bridge,* which means "safe crossing" in Chinese. Considering the Anji has stood for 1,400 years, it's a very good name!

SPANNING TIME

At bridge construction sites today, backhoes dig huge pits for foundations, and bulldozers move mounds of dirt. Tall cranes lift beams into place, and heavy mechanical hammers force posts into the ground. Dump trucks and flatbeds bring load after load of heavy materials from far away.

When the Anji Bridge was completed, there were no bulldozers or backhoes, no cranes or flatbed trucks. The wooden carts the Chinese had were too small to carry the massive stones used to make the arch. So the Chinese did what the Romans and Egyptians had done before them. They used what they had. The Chinese workers took advantage of their cold winters, pouring water on the path between the quarry and the bridge site. Once the water froze, they slid the stones over the slippery ice!

See What Li Chun Saw

Trace around a large bowl and a small one on a piece of paper; cut out the two circles.

Fold the small circle in half and cut along the fold.

Use the straight edge of one half-circle like a ruler to measure across the large circle. Draw a line across the large circle so the distance across equals the length of the small circle's straight edge. Cut along the line. The smaller piece of the large circle is a shallow arch.

Compare your shallow and semicircular arches. Are their lengths the same? Which is flatter? Try making an arch that's the same height but longer than your shallow arch.

To show the pushing force, draw arrows from the top of your paper arches down along the curved edges to the ends. Do the arrows point in the same direction when they reach the ends? Would you build abutments in the same way for the two types of arches? (The abutments keep the arch from spreading outward.) Where would a shallow arch need more support than a semicircular arch? If you said on the sides, you'd be correct.

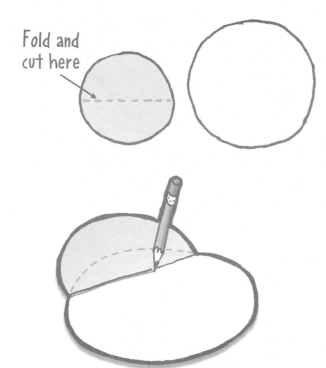

Fold and cut here

Flood Control

The Chinese believed that special dragons could protect bridges from floods. According to legend, their huge mouths would devour the gushing waters of a flood and save the bridge.

See if you can discover what really saved the Anji Bridge from floods.

Anji Bridge Shape

Find a rectangular cake pan. Measure its height and width; then, cut two rectangles with the same dimensions from poster board. On one piece draw a shallow-arch bridge in the shape of the Anji Bridge. Cut it out, and use it to trace a second bridge on the other piece of poster board. Cut that out, too.

Stand one of the bridges on the bottom of the pan so it reaches from side to side. Lightly tape the arch to the pan's sides. Then, pour water into the pan to just below the level of the arch's opening.

Carefully tip the pan back and forth to create a flood. What happens to the arch? Where does the water flow?

Empty the pan and dry the inside. Cut holes in your second arch where the Anji has holes. Tape it to the pan and add water to the same level as before. Now create a flood again. Where does the water flow?

Thinking about the forces that water puts on a bridge, how do you think these inner arches function during floods?

Test Which Arch Is Stronger

Test the strength of two arch bridges. Both will have the roadway on top of the arch. One will have vertical supports like some steel arch bridges; the other will have no supporting columns.

Start by cutting poster board into these bridge parts:

← **Arches: Two strips 2" X 14" (5 cm X 35 cm)**
↙ **Decks: Two strips 2" X 11" (5 cm X 25 cm)**
↓ **Piers: Four strips 2" X 4" (5 cm X 10 cm)**

You'll also need two heavy books for abutments, coins for load, and tape.

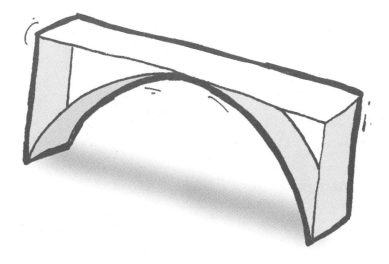

Tape the center of one deck strip to the center of one arch strip. Tape a pier between the ends of the deck and arch at both sides. This will cause the longer strip to curve into an arch. Be sure not to bend any of the strips.

 continued

Make a second bridge just like the first. Add supports by tap-ing short pieces of poster board between the deck and the arch.

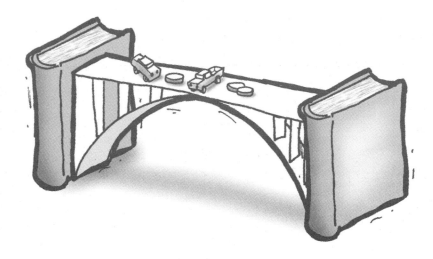

Place the books on a table about 11 inches (25 cm) apart. Then, put the bridges in between them, one behind the other. Now test their strengths by adding the same kind of coins, one at a time, to each bridge.

And the winner is …? Which bridge can hold more load before sagging? Are the arches you made semicircular or shallow?

Take The Challenge!

The Job:
You've been hired to design a bridge with four lanes for cars and trucks, and two train tracks across a river that's about 1,500 feet (450 m) wide.

The Site:
The bridge site lies between the ocean and the city's harbor. The river is very deep and very busy with freighters and many other boats. The banks are rocky from the bottom of the river to halfway up the shore, and the banks are sandy closer to ground level. The rolling hills in the far distance seem to match the waves of the ocean.

The Challenges:
The currents in the river are tricky, and boats need a lot of room from side to side. City officials want the bridge built as quickly as possible for as little money as possible. But they also want a bridge that's interesting and nice to look at.

Things to Consider:
In choosing the main materials, consider how strong the bridge needs to be as well as how long. Also, think about where you can put abutments and whether you can use piers in the middle.

Will you accept the challenge? We know you can do this — and do it very well at that!

The Beam Bridge:
SIMPLE but STRONG

Next time you're driving along a highway, count how many times you go over or under a bridge that carries one road over another. You'll notice lots of beam bridges. They're simple in design, and easier and less expensive to build than other kinds of bridges.

Beam bridges also solve lots of problems. A part of the New Jersey Turnpike, for instance, is a beam bridge that carries the pike over wet, swampy land that's too soft to support a regular highway. It also reduces damage to the marshland from the highway.

But beam bridges can't do everything. They can't be made tall enough and can't always reach far enough to let very large ships pass beneath them. A long beam bridge, after all, is really just a lot of shorter beam bridges, or spans, joined together and supported by piers.

HOW THE BEAM BRIDGE CAME TO BE

So how were the first long wooden beam bridges invented? Well, think about the last time you crossed a stream where there wasn't a bridge. Perhaps you laid a log across the water. That's most likely how the first beam bridges were born.

Later, somebody split logs to make the first flat, wide deck. Someone saw the ends sinking into the muddy shores and put rocks under them, making the first abutments. Eventually, people realized you could pile rocks in the middle of wide streams and use planks on both sides to reach the shores.

A Fast-Forward History of London Bridge

Yes, the famous London Bridge began its life as a wooden beam bridge. It was built, destroyed, and rebuilt so many times, people almost lost count! Can you figure it out?

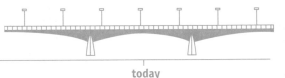

start Romansbuiltfirstbridgeacross Thames Riverdestroyedreplaced Vikingscametwicedestroyedagain infloodsfires destroyedotherwoodenbridgerebuilt littleun tilgreatstonebridgecompleted1209called Old London Bridgewith19 archesevenstoresunbelievabledraw bridgetowerbut fires damagedsofivearchbridgeputupthentaken downnewconcretebridgewith three arches sixtrafficlanesstandstoday.

Make a London Bridge Flip Book

| 1209 | 1831 | today |

Here's a cool way to illustrate your own fast-action story of London Bridge's historic "ups and downs." Staple together about 20 index cards or pieces of scrap paper (4" x 6"/ 10 cm x 15 cm).

Start the story on the last page by drawing a simple picture of the beginning of the story near the bottom of the page. Flip to the next-to-last page, and make a second drawing that continues the action of the first drawing. Don't make the drawing too different from the first, or it'll seem to skip too fast. Continue forward to each page of your story, drawing pictures for at least 20 pages. Add details and color when finished. Then, flip through your book from back to front, and watch the ups and downs of the London Bridge in action!

THE STORY BEHIND THE RHYME

London Bridge is falling down, falling down, falling down,
London Bridge is falling down, my fair lady.

We've all sung this rhyme, but how did it get started? Some historians think it began 1,000 years ago when the English and Norwegian armies battled the Danish Vikings. The London Bridge separated the two warring sides. When the English couldn't cross the bridge or row their boats under it to attack the Danish fort on the other side, they tied ropes around the bridge's wooden supports and rowed their boats as hard as they could downstream. The bridge came tumbling down! Other historians believe the rhyme got its start after ice knocked down five of the bridge's arches in 1281.

⚙ HOW IT WORKS! ⚙

Triangles are very rigid, or stiff, shapes. The great thing about triangles is they don't change when a force is applied, because their shape helps spread the force evenly around the sides. That property makes the triangle a terrific building block when it comes to building bridges.

Trestles and Triangles

Julius Caesar, the Roman leader, bragged in his diaries that it took his army only 10 days to build a long trestle bridge (a beam bridge with supports that slant) over the Rhine River in western Europe. When he had no more use for the bridge, he had it destroyed!

Find two pencils and stick them into a cardboard box so the erasers slant toward each other like the piles, or piers, of a Roman trestle bridge. Push the erasers so they touch in a triangle shape. That's the shape of the trestle.

Why use a triangle for the trestle bridge? You'll need seven straight straws (the kind that don't bend) and straight pins. Make a square by pinning the ends of four straws together. Use three straws to make a triangle. Gently push and pull on the square and triangle. Which one holds its shape best?

Testing Triangles for Strength

Using wood glue, connect three Popsicle sticks together into a triangle. Then, add two sticks to one side of it to make another triangle (this one will be upside down). Make another one next to that triangle for three triangles in a row. After the glue dries, wiggle it. Is it rigid?

Hey, you've made what bridge builders call a truss, a framework made by joining straight pieces into triangles. Trusses are used in bridges to add strength and stability. Truss-beam bridges are made by connecting two trusses on either side with beams across the top and bottom. The deck lies on the bottom crossbeams. The whole thing can be put together on shore before being lifted onto piers, making it very easy to build.

YAY!

YAY!

KANSAS STATE

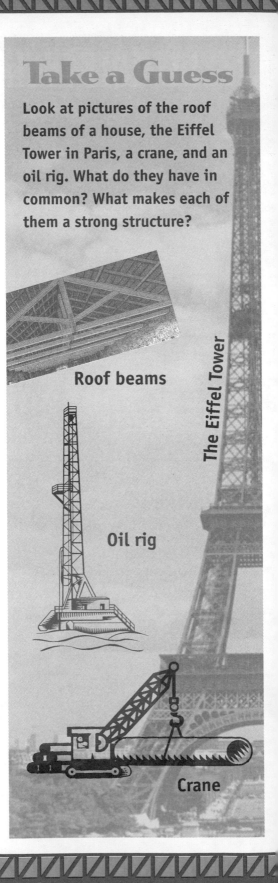

Take a Guess

Look at pictures of the roof beams of a house, the Eiffel Tower in Paris, a crane, and an oil rig. What do they have in common? What makes each of them a strong structure?

Roof beams

The Eiffel Tower

Oil rig

Crane

Build an Amazing Truss Bridge

You'll need lots of Popsicle sticks and lots of patience to make this bridge, but the end result is worth it! You'll also need some wood glue, two heavy books, a ruler, string, hole punch, rocks, and a small plastic container such as a yogurt cup.

1. *Make two trusses like the one shown. For each one, use four Popsicle sticks along the bottom, three along the top, and one on each side. Make sure the bottom and top are straight. After they dry, glue six Popsicle sticks to each frame to make the triangles inside, and let dry.*

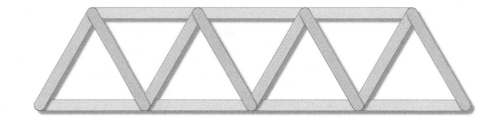

2. *Lean the trusses in between heavy books, about one Popsicle stick apart. If they fall towards the middle, put a heavy object at the base of each one. Connect them by gluing four sticks across the top where the triangles come to a point. After they dry, remove the books. Glue five sticks across the bottom, putting two at the ends and three where the upside-down triangles come to a point. These are your crossbeams. Once again, let everything dry.*

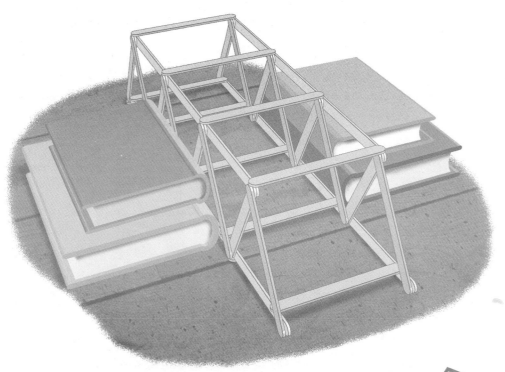

continued

3. *Test your bridge by wiggling it. Does it move a lot or is it sturdy? To increase its stiffness, add pieces that crisscross over the top beams, and let dry. (You'll have to glue two sticks together to make long enough pieces.)*

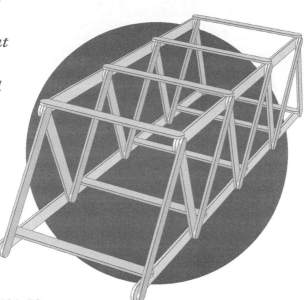

The Forces in a Truss

Some parts of a truss bridge are squeezed (under compression), some are stretched (put under tension), and some are under both forces. In general, the top of a truss is compressed and the bottom is tensed. The pieces in between may be under just one or both forces.

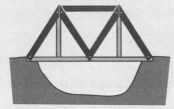

■ COMPRESSION (SQUEEZED)
■ TENSION (STRETCHED)

4. *Stand the books up to use as piers at the ends of the bridge, and lay a ruler on the bottom crossbeams. Punch two holes on the opposite sides of the plastic container, and hang it from the ruler. Add rocks and other small, heavy things to the container. Can you add enough load to make the bridge squeak, sag, or wiggle? If not, stack books on top of the bridge until it does. What part gives way first? How could you make it stronger?*

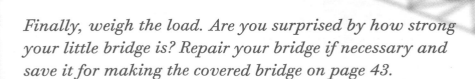

Finally, weigh the load. Are you surprised by how strong your little bridge is? Repair your bridge if necessary and save it for making the covered bridge on page 43.

Cover Your Bridge

With just a few Popsicle sticks, you can transform your truss bridge into an old-fashioned covered bridge. Use Popsicle sticks for siding and a piece of folded cardboard for the roof. Then give it a layer of poster paint — "barn red" would look nice.

Good Question!

Many covered bridges, especially long ones, combined the truss and the arch. Based on what you know about arches, why do you think an arch was included?

PEOPLE
MAKE IT HAPPEN

The Tale of the First Covered Bridge

It's said that around 1800 or so, **Judge Richard Peters** was asked to build a permanent bridge across the Schuylkill (skoo-kill) River in Philadelphia to replace the rickety *pontoon* (floating) *bridge* that was there. He started with stone piers, but taking advantage of available resources, the judge used wood for the bridge and hired carpenter Timothy Palmer to design a truss beam.

Still, something just didn't sit right with Judge Peters, even as they were about to finish the *Schuylkill River Bridge*. Each season of the year presented its own problems for the bridge: spring rains, hot summers, slippery autumn leaves, and winter's snow and ice. Under such conditions, a wooden bridge was sure to rot quickly.

So Judge Peters told Palmer to cover it up. That would surely make it last forever. Well, almost, anyway!

PEOPLE MAKE IT HAPPEN

Squire Whipple

The Father of Iron Bridges

In 1841, **Squire Whipple** built his first iron bridge, the *Erie Canal Bridge* in New York State, using two kinds of iron, cast iron and wrought iron. He'd determined that cast iron was stronger for the bridge parts under compression, while wrought iron was stronger in tension.

Whipple wrote a book explaining all he'd learned about the forces in a truss and how to measure them. His work turned bridge building into a science and made it possible to use math to figure out the best sizes and shapes of the parts of a truss.

In America, Whipple became known as the "Father of Iron Bridges." Because of his work, other bridge builders could test their designs on paper before building them.

From Wood to Iron

Why did we turn to iron for railway bridges? One bridge story provides the answer. In 1836, the *Harpers Ferry Bridge*, a wooden truss, was built across the Potomac River in West Virginia. At the time, steam locomotives were so small, they would look like an amusement park ride to us today. But the "Iron Horse," as locomotives were called, quickly grew larger and more powerful.

The problem wasn't that wooden trusses couldn't carry the weight. The challenge was building a bridge that could take *a heavy weight in motion all of a sudden*. The train made the bridge shake like crazy. Wooden parts often gave way under all the wear and tear.

So iron parts were added to the truss designs. By 1851, that wooden truss bridge at Harpers Ferry was groaning under the trains. It was replaced with an iron bridge strong enough to hold up three enormous locomotives.

What Went Wrong?

In the mid-1800s, America was racing to connect the East and West Coasts. As track was laid length by length, bridges were quickly built. And as quickly as bridges were going up, it seemed they were coming down.

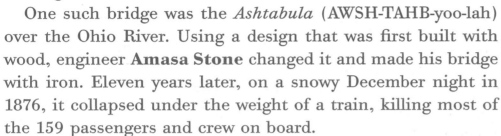

LEARNING FROM
DISASTERS!

One such bridge was the *Ashtabula* (AWSH-TAHB-yoo-lah) over the Ohio River. Using a design that was first built with wood, engineer **Amasa Stone** changed it and made his bridge with iron. Eleven years later, on a snowy December night in 1876, it collapsed under the weight of a train, killing most of the 159 passengers and crew on board.

The whole country was shaken by the disaster. People became afraid to ride on trains. Railroad companies sat up and took notice. They realized that trains had gotten too heavy for their bridges, so they changed the type of iron used in bridge construction. They sought advice on new designs from engineers and other experts, and a new specialty of *civil engineer* — the bridge engineer — was born. These efforts helped make train travel safer.

Think About It

Do the Eyes Have It?

Only a few iron truss bridges built before 1860 still survive. Many were destroyed during the Civil War, some were torn down for scrap metal during World Wars I and II, and still others simply collapsed.

But some people believe we haven't saved them because they're not as impressive as suspension bridges, or as graceful as stone arches, or as pretty as a covered bridge.

Is the art of *historic preservation* only about preserving beauty, or is it about preserving our history, too?

DO YOU HAVE GEPHYROPHOBIA?

Are you afraid of crossing bridges? Many people are. There's even a long name for such a fear — gephyrophobia. Most people have fears about something, often of things they don't understand. What might you do to help someone overcome a fear of bridges?

Write a Bridge Poem

American poet Walt Whitman was inspired by the beauty of bridges and America's drive to join its land.

"The Earth be spanned, connected by network.
The lands be welded together."
— Walt Whitman

Write a poem or a story about bridges and how they connect the land and people. Perhaps you'll write about a wooden bridge that's served long and hard, and is at the end of its days.

Like Whitman, try to use the language of bridges as you write. Notice the word "welded," which means joining pieces of metal using heat. Imagine what it was like in 1869 when the Union Pacific and Central Pacific Railroads were finally linked across America. Such a network of tracks, bridges, and tunnels would certainly have seemed to span the earth, joining the land together.

Courageous Kate!

On the dark and stormy night of July 6, 1881, in Iowa, 15-year-old Kate Shelley put aside her fears. Nearby, Honey Creek was already flooding, and Kate knew the Des Moines River would, too, threatening the railroad bridge. She also knew a train was due any minute. Racing against time, with only flashes of lightning to light her way, she crawled across the wooden bridge as water flowed over it. She made it! Just in time, she stopped the train and saved its 200 passengers.

Create a Cantilever

Where does a ruler need to be for it to balance on your finger? In the middle! At that point, the two sides of the ruler weigh the same. They serve as counterweights to each other, just like two children of the same weight on a balanced seesaw.

Next, try balancing the ruler near one of its ends. What happens? The longer, heavier side keeps tilting down, doesn't it? Try again, this time putting a finger on top of the short end. Like magic, it balances! The first finger is the support, *the second is the* counterweight, *and the ruler is the* cantilever. *Because it's made of a stiff material, it sticks straight out.*

A cantilever bridge works the same way. It takes advantage of the stiffness of a beam's material and the ability to balance a beam on one support.

THE STEELY FORTH

As the railroad companies scrambled to make their bridges safer, locomotives continued to grow. The "Iron Horse" had become an "Iron Monster." The railroads realized they needed the strength of steel.

Scotland's gigantic *Forth Bridge* was the first long-span railroad bridge made only of steel. The bridge crossed a wide waterway called the Firth of Forth. (How's that for a tongue-twister!) Upon its completion in 1890, it broke all the records. Its span was the longest of any bridge, and it was the tallest. It also used a new design inspired by the simple cantilever, which is a beam that projects beyond its single support, as a branch coming out of a tree trunk.

The fame of the Forth is that it took the design to the extreme and still kept the bridge strong. For more than 100 years, it has stood up against bad weather and heavy train traffic.

Forth Bridge • Scotland • 1890

Try This! *Cut three long strips of stiff cardboard all the same size, and two short strips with the same width as the long pieces. Cut a paper towel tube into three equal pieces. Balance the long strips on the tubes, and lay the short strips in between the cantilever arms. Does your bridge need abutments?*

⚙ HOW IT WORKS! ⚙

A simple cantilever bridge has two cantilevers. One end of each cantilever is held down by an abutment that acts as a counterweight. The other ends, or arms, reach out towards each other and meet in the center. A single pier supports each cantilever.

To make the bridge longer, a short beam can be hung in between the cantilevers. An even longer bridge — just like the Forth — can be made by adding cantilevers in the middle, each balancing itself as the ruler did when you supported it in the middle.

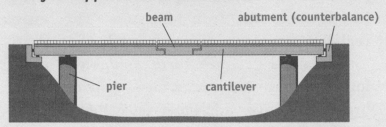

Be a Living Bridge

Benjamin Baker's demonstration of why a cantilever bridge is safe.

The Firth of Forth is not far from where the *Tay Bridge* in Scotland had collapsed in 1879. Heavy winds and the weight of a train brought the Tay down; because of the disaster and the use of the cantilever, people were suspicious of the Forth Bridge.

To convince people that such an odd-looking bridge would be safe, one of its designers, **Benjamin Baker**, went around giving a living demonstration. He had two men on chairs support a third man in between them on a seat. They used short poles to hold up the seat and to reach the ropes attached to piles of bricks. The men's arms were in tension, as were the ropes, and the chair legs and the poles were being compressed.

Look at the picture carefully. Can you figure out a way to make your own "living" bridge? Just be sure the person in the middle is small!

Cheapest Is Not Always Best

In less than 15 seconds, the *Quebec Bridge* that crossed the St. Lawrence River near Quebec City in Canada came crashing down on August 29, 1907. Its problems began 10 years earlier when there wasn't enough money to start building the bridge. Engineer **Theodore Cooper** chose a cantilever design because he said it was the "cheapest and best."

The river was deep and wide, and in the winter, big chunks of ice floated on it. Cooper changed the bridge's design to make the center span 200 feet (61 m) longer. This allowed piers to be in shallow water near the shores and away from the ice. They would be easier and cheaper to build, too. But Cooper didn't use the weight of the longer span in figuring out the stress on the bridge, because he thought the change wouldn't make a difference.

Weeks before the collapse, the extra weight caused parts of the bridge to bend. Engineers alerted Cooper to the problem, but he didn't go to Quebec to see for himself. Work continued, and the parts bent more. Finally, Cooper ordered the work to stop. But before they could be warned, workers on the bridge heard a grinding sound, then loud noises like cannon fire. Steel beams ripped apart and cables snapped. Nineteen thousand tons of cantilevers and spans thundered into the St. Lawrence, crushing and drowning 75 men.

EEEERK... DINK! BOING! BOP!

Did He Know Better?

At the time of the Quebec Bridge disaster, Cooper was the most famous builder of railroad bridges in North America. Earlier in his career, he had written articles that advised bridge builders to calculate stresses carefully, test materials for strength, and inspect bridges as they were built. But Cooper also believed in an engineer's *instincts*, a gut feeling that says you're right.

Think about a time when you went with your gut instinct and did what you felt was right. Did it turn out OK? When is it a good time to follow your gut, and when should you follow rules and procedures?

FROM TRUSSES TO GIRDERS

Though trusses are still used today, more often, modern bridges use beams called *girders* that are shaped in special ways to make them strong. One type, the *I-beam*, looks like a capital "I" from the end. The *plate girder* looks like a more complex I-beam. Plate girders are stronger than I-beams and can be used to make longer bridges.

Confederation Bridge

As the huge crane dropped the last box girder span into place on November 19, 1996, the crane's operator shouted, "We have touchdown." The wide and icy Northumberland Strait between Prince Edward Island and New Brunswick in Canada had finally been bridged. The world's longest bridge over ice-covered waters, the *Confederation Bridge*, is 8 miles (12.9 km) long, including its approaches, and is made up of two types of concrete box girders. The connections between long and short girders are hinged on one side so if ice or a ship crashes into the bridge only that section will be damaged.

Still curious about the Confederation Bridge? Then check out its Web site: http://www.confederationbridge.com.html

An example of "booming up" an I-beam.

Learn the Lingo

When a crane operator raises or lowers the end of the crane to lift or lower steel beams, engineers call it *"booming up"* and *"booming down."*

Connecting a beam or other piece of the bridge structure to the crane's cable so it can be hoisted, or lifted, into place is called *rigging*.

The Confederation Bridge (under construction)

SPANNING TIME

The first link to the mainland (New Brunswick) from Prince Edward Island was by iceboat. The trip cost just $2 one way. But passengers didn't always get their money's worth. If the wind wasn't strong, they'd have to get out and push!

In 1917 the first ferry service started, and soon it became a part of the quiet and peaceful life on Prince Edward. People relaxed on the boat, watching the sunset and letting their hair blow in the wind.

With the opening of the Confederation Bridge, the ferry to New Brunswick closed. Now people drive across the strait in 10 minutes for $35. Concrete guardrails protect travelers from the wind, but, unfortunately, they're so high, no one can see the beautiful view around them.

Pros & Cons

Many islanders fear the Confederation Bridge will change life on Prince Edward Island. They worry about more traffic, tourists, and development. On the other hand, some islanders welcome the bridge and the changes it will bring.

What kind of changes would you expect to see on the island now that the bridge exists? What could you do to help maintain the quiet life of the island, while enjoying the convenience and opportunities brought about by the building of the bridge?

It's a real dilemma — how to preserve what is special, and also make progress and bring economic health to an area.

Take The Challenge!

The Job:
The size of the job is staggering. You're hired to build a railroad bridge across a valley that's nearly a mile (1.6 km) wide.

The Site:
A narrow river runs through the deep valley where a few farmers live. The bedrock is fairly close to the surface.

The Challenges:
You need to keep the train in a level position as it crosses the deep valley. Many piers will be needed and they'll have to be tall. However, you don't want heavy piers or so many that they interfere too much with the farms below. All modern materials are available.

Things to Consider:
Start with the piers. They have to be sturdy because the bridge will carry trains, and they have to be tall. What material and design will work best? Think about what kind of beams will provide both strength and length for the deck. Trusses? Girders? What should they be made of? Should you be concerned with how the bridge will look?

FROM THREADS IN THE SKY:
Suspension Bridges

Newport Bridge • Newport, RI • 1969

Suspension bridges amaze everybody, even the engineers who build them. No other kind of bridge gives us quite the same feeling. From a distance, they look fragile, hanging from thin threads you can barely see. Even as we admire them, we wonder how they stay up.

Modern suspension bridges might look fragile, but they're very strong, thanks to their design and the materials used to build them. Like arches and beam bridges, they balance the forces of tension and compression.

Hang a Bridge

Hanging bridges had their beginnings in South America, Africa, and Asia. Thousands of years ago, people hung cables from trees on one side of a river or canyon to join to trees on the other side. Cables were fashioned by twisting vines. (Unravel a piece of twine to see how they made them.) You've probably seen hanging bridges in adventure movies that take place in the jungles and rain forests. To make your own outdoor hanging bridge, you'll need two sturdy trees quite near each other, twigs, rope, twine, and scissors.

1. *To make handrails, tie one end of the rope to a tree. Loop the rope around the other tree, and then bring it back to the first tree and tie it. The rope should be taut.*

2. *Put up another piece of rope underneath the first in the same way. This rope should droop a little. Make sure the ropes hang evenly.*

3. *To make the footpath, tie the twigs into bundles and lay them across the lower ropes. With twine, tie the handrail ropes to the twigs and lower ropes on both sides.*

continued

4. *Put some load, such as big rocks or a bucket filled with dirt or water, on your bridge. Can you see the tension in the rope and twine? Are any parts being compressed? If it seems sturdy enough, try it out yourself. Just be sure the ground underneath is soft!*

IRON-CHAIN BRIDGES

Iron moved the suspension bridge out of the vine-and-twig stage. The first iron suspension bridge had two iron chains slung over piers and secured at both ends in the ground beyond them. The chains drooped in the middle. The deck was hung from the chains with iron rods. Sound familiar? It's the same as a simple hanging bridge.

Even before the first major iron-chain bridge was completed in 1826, however, other bridge builders were substituting wrought-iron wire, woven into cables, for the chains and rods. Because the cables were continuous, they were stronger in tension than chains that could break at the links. Soon chains were out and wire was in.

Making It Safe

When it came time to bid on building a bridge crossing the rugged gorge just below Niagara Falls that would link the railroads of the United States and Canada, **John Roebling** lost the bid to **Charles Ellet**. But when Ellet couldn't finish his bridge, Roebling came to the railroad's rescue. For four years, he and his workers fought disease and bad weather, but the completed *Niagara Bridge* was worth the effort. Trains rumbled across its upper deck and horse-drawn carriages trotted along its lower one.

While Roebling was being hailed for his Niagara Bridge, Ellet's career took a nosedive. His *Wheeling Bridge*, in West Virginia, plunged into the Ohio River in 1854, while being whipped into a twisting frenzy by a storm. Ellet never again built a major bridge, while Roebling went on to become the most famous bridge builder in the world. What made the difference?

Roebling was always observing the world around him; he was ready to apply what he learned to improve his own work. He learned an important lesson from the Wheeling disaster: The major weakness of suspension bridges was their lack of stability and stiffness. The

bridge's flexible deck allowed it to whip around in the wind. Yet, years later, engineers ignored his findings and built the Tacoma Narrows Bridge that would also twist to destruction in the wind (see page 64).

But Roebling applied the lesson: He stiffened the Niagara Bridge with wooden trusses between the decks and added *stays*, cables from the towers to the decks and from the decks to the rocky cliffs. The Niagara lasted until locomotives got too heavy for its iron cables. In 1897 it was taken down and replaced by a steel arch. By then, Roebling had already shown the world that long suspended spans could carry heavy loads.

MARK TWAIN'S VIEWS

Not everyone was convinced the Niagara Bridge was safe. Mark Twain wrote that when on the bridge, fear was divided between "the chances of smashing down 200 feet (61.5 m) into the river below, and the chances of having a railway train overhead smashing down on you."

Steel and the Brooklyn Bridge

Steel and suspension bridges first came together in the building of the *Brooklyn Bridge* over the East River in New York. And who was the bridge engineer who would bring this newest material into suspension bridge cable design? None other than John Roebling!

The Brooklyn Bridge was remarkable for many reasons. One was simply its length of nearly 1,600 feet (488 m), but another was the awe-inspiring height of its gray granite towers. To make such a long, tall bridge, Roebling and his son Washington developed new ways of spinning cables and putting in foundations that are still used today.

Brooklyn Bridge • Brooklyn, NY • 1883

HOW IT WORKS!

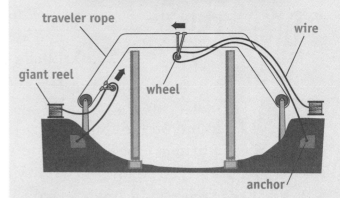

traveler rope • giant reel • wheel • wire • anchor

To spin steel into cables, steel is drawn, or pulled, into wire as thick as a pencil. The wire is then wound around giant reels (like thread on a spool) that are set up near the anchors at the bridge site.

The first wire is usually ferried across the body of water by boat. Workers on top of the towers lift that wire and then pull up a second one. The two are looped over pulleys at the anchors and joined to make a *traveler rope*. Special wheels are attached to it.

The loose end of the wire from a reel is secured to an anchor and looped around each wheel. As the traveler rope moves, the wheels carry the wires over the towers from anchor to anchor. The whole thing works like a spider spinning its web.

When a certain number of wires have been laid, the workers bind them into a *strand*, like a bunch of pencils held in your hand. Groups of strands are then squeezed and wrapped into *cables*. In the Brooklyn Bridge, each strand has 286 wires and each cable has 19 strands (19 x 286 = 5,434 wires).

Spin a Cable

Find a piece of rope, a spool of thread, and two chairs. Place the chairs back-to-back about a giant step apart. Tie a loop of rope around the chairs, and pull the loop so the knot is near one chair. Tie the end of the thread to that chair. Now hook the thread over the knot. Pull the rope so the knot moves to the other chair, pulling the thread with it. How many threads span the distance between the chairs? How could you get four threads across?

Thread loops around knot

How Many Wires?

The number of wires in each strand, the number of strands in each cable, and the number of cables differ for each suspension bridge. The Brooklyn Bridge has four cables, each containing 5,434 wires. The Golden Gate Bridge in San Francisco has two cables, each with 27,572 wires. So, for all you math wizards, how many more wires are in each Golden Gate cable than in each Brooklyn Bridge cable? Why do you think there is this difference (answer below)?

ANSWER: There are 22,138 more wires in each cable of the Golden Gate Bridge. The Golden Gate Bridge is more than 2 1/2 times longer than the Brooklyn Bridge, so it's heavier and needs stronger cables.

Learn the Lingo

Workers who dug at the bottom of the caissons were nicknamed *sand hogs*. Imagine going to work each day at the bottom of this underwater structure! Sand hogs were also in charge of *dewatering* (pumping water out of) the caissons. What a tough job the sand hogs had.

Air Keeps the Water Out

Fill a large bowl with water and push a small glass upside down straight into the water. Try standing the glass on the bottom without holding it. It can't be done, because there's air inside. The air doesn't let the water come into the glass all the way. Tilt the glass and watch the air bubbles escape. Now will the glass stand on the bottom?

SPANNING TIME

The Brooklyn Bridge was the first suspension bridge to use caissons instead of cofferdams (see page 29). A *caisson* is a huge box or tube usually made of concrete or steel (the Brooklyn Bridge used wooden ones). They're tall enough to reach from the water's surface to the riverbed. Only the bottom is open.

Today, large cranes are used to dig out the rocks, mud, and sand. But, on the Brooklyn Bridge, workmen did the digging in a room at the bottom of the caisson. Air was forced into the room under high pressure to keep the water out. Meanwhile, other workers built the stone pier on top of the caisson, which pushed it deeper and deeper into the riverbed. When a caisson reaches bedrock, the concrete foundation is poured (using waterproof concrete, of course), and the pier or tower is completed.

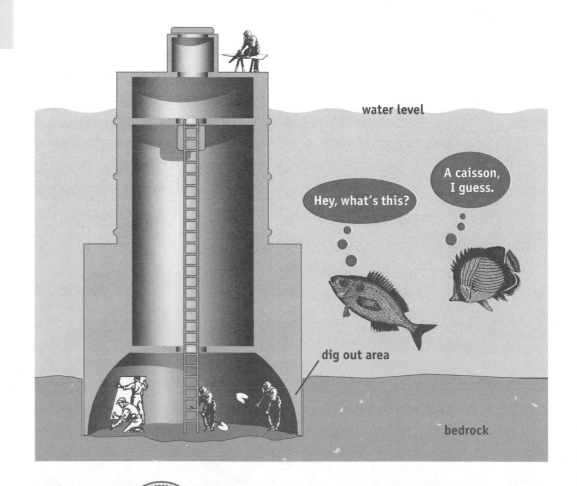

water level

Hey, what's this?

A caisson, I guess.

dig out area

bedrock

PEOPLE
MAKE IT HAPPEN

The Roeblings: A Family of Builders

John Roebling

Washington Roebling

Emily Roebling

It took three Roeblings to build the Brooklyn Bridge — a father, a son, and a wife. The Brooklyn Bridge was John Roebling's dream. But when Roebling first suggested a long suspension bridge between Manhattan and Brooklyn in 1867, other engineers thought it couldn't be done. So Roebling spent the next two years planning every detail and checking every calculation twice.

When Roebling again presented his plan, the engineers were forced to agree it would be strong and safe. Unfortunately, John Roebling didn't live to make his dream come true. Just weeks after getting the go-ahead, his right foot was crushed in an accident at the bridge site. Doctors amputated his toes, but his foot became infected, and he died.

His son **Washington**, also an engineer and bridge builder, took over his dream. It took 14 years to build the Brooklyn Bridge. The most difficult were the first three miserable years spent in the caissons. As the caissons went deeper, the dreaded bends (an illness caused by moving quickly from high pressure in deep water to normal pressure) caused three sand hogs to die. Many others got sick. And so did Washington. Confined to his bed, Washington could no longer go to the site. Another Roebling — Washington's wife, Emily — picked up the dream.

Although not an engineer, **Emily Warren Roebling** quickly learned the language of bridges and became an expert in bridge construction. She met with engineers at the site, telling them her husband's ideas and instructions. Then she'd return to Washington's bedside, bringing him news and questions. It was Emily who, as the "voice of her husband," oversaw the completion of the Brooklyn Bridge. The Roeblings, working together, made their dream come true.

Make a Blueprint

John Roebling died before the Brooklyn Bridge got underway, yet his son was able to carry on because his plans were so detailed. Part of a builder's plans are a set of blueprints, or drawings, that show exactly how the structure should be built and how it will look when it's done. There are measurements on the drawings showing the size of the different parts.

Ask a grown-up in your family if they have blueprints for the house or apartment where you live. Examine the drawings with them. Can you find your bedroom? How about the stairs and windows?

Now, you draw a blueprint (on graph paper if you have any) for a bridge, a tower, or a floor of a house. Then, see if you can follow your plan and build your structure with blocks, cardboard, Popsicle sticks, or whatever is handy.

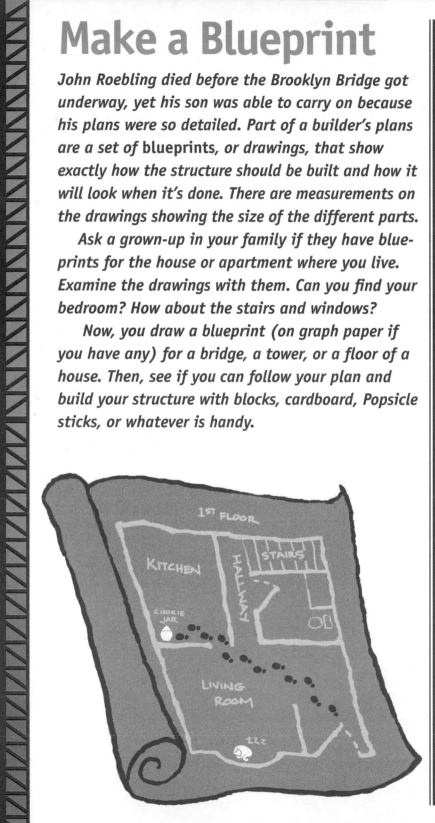

Hang a Suspension Bridge

Materials:

⬅ 2 kitchen chairs with space above the seats
↙ Spool of heavy string
↓ 4 heavy books
↘ Masking tape
➡ Cardboard
↗ Scissors and hole punch
↑ Spool of thread (or light string)

1. *Set up your towers (the chairs) on a rug. The foundation of your bridge will be the floor. Place the chairs back-to-back, as far apart as your arms can reach.*

Tie the end of the heavy string to a book, ich will act as an anchor. Put the book on one ir. Loop the string around the top of the chair d bring it to the other chair. Loop the string und the top of that chair, letting it sag in a ve between the chairs.

Cut the string and tie it around another book. the book on the other chair. Push this string to side of the chairs. Make another cable in the ne way on the other side. Tie it to the same

books as the other one, making sure the two cables are even. The strings between the books and the chairs should be tight. If the string slips off the chairs, tape it in place.

4. Cut and tape cardboard to make a roadway long enough to reach farther than from book to book. It should be slightly wider than the distance between the cables. Lay the deck in place on the books, and put a third book on top.

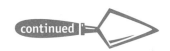 continued

5. *For hangers, tie pieces of thread along the length of both cables. Make them long enough so they hang below the deck.*

6. *Punch holes along the edge of the deck where the hangers fall; then, thread a hanger through each hole. Tie them so the hangers are taut and the cardboard deck is level.*

Now, put load on your bridge. Can you see the tension in the cables and hangers? Does the string get tight? Do the anchors (books) move? If they do, how could you keep them in place? Does the deck sag? If it does, how could you make it stiffer? Test your bridge in the wind by putting a fan next to it and blowing air at it at different speeds. Are you concerned about how much your bridge wiggles or waves in the wind? Think of ways to use cables to help stabilize it.

The Driving Force

Just as trains did in the 1800s, cars in the 1900s made new demands on bridges and bridge builders. Henry Ford introduced the first affordable car, the Model T, in 1908. By 1930, there were 27 million cars on North American roads. Arch and beam bridges went up by the thousands to take care of narrow rivers and highway overpasses, but what about wide waterways around cities like New York and San Francisco? They could only be spanned by suspension bridges.

When New York's *George Washington Bridge* opened in 1931, it more than doubled the length of the previous longest span. Its designer, **Othmar Ammann**, had argued for years with the city about building a bridge over the Hudson River to New Jersey. Once again others said it couldn't be done. But like John Roebling, Ammann was a daring man, willing to try things that hadn't been done before. Not only did he get his bridge built, but he designed it for cars, with one-way entrances and exits, to make it easy for lots of traffic to get on and off.

Where's Othmar when you need 'im?

Think About It

A Future Vision

Looking to the future is very important when you are spending huge sums of money to build a structure as monumental as a bridge. You have to imagine what will come later. What did Othmar Ammann see when he looked into the future? More traffic! So he provided space on the first deck of the George Washington Bridge for extra lanes and made the towers and cables strong enough for a second deck. The second deck was added in 1962.

When you look to the future, what kinds of things do you imagine that we as a world population should be planning for? Do you and your friends have concerns about our planet's future? Now is the time to begin planning and speaking out for the changes you foresee.

Although It Galloped, It Wasn't a Horse

Tacoma Narrows Bridge • Seattle, Washington • 1940

Nicknamed "Galloping Gertie," the original *Tacoma Narrows Bridge* rippled up and down like a roller coaster. People drove across just for fun; others got motion sickness just crossing it. It was a long and very narrow bridge that crossed the Puget Sound south of Seattle, Washington. It was also the most flexible modern suspension bridge ever built.

On November 7, 1940, when the bridge was only 4 months old, a 40-mph (64-kmh) wind blew and the waters of the sound were whipped into whitecaps. The bridge began to wave more than usual. Finally, the waves got so big, traffic was stopped. Without warning, the deck began twisting violently.

Then, with a loud roar, part of the center span tore away from its cables, flipped over, and plunged into the churning water below. A side beam ripped away from the deck like a zipper. Huge chunks of concrete flew into the air "like popcorn," said one witness. Only torn and tangled pieces of the span remained attached to the buckled and bent steel towers. Want to see for yourself? Visit the bridge disaster at the Web site:

http://www.nwwf.com/wa003a.htm

See Why Tacoma Tumbled

Cut two long strips of paper, one about 2 inches (5 cm) wide, the other about 4 inches (10 cm) wide. Place them on a table. Hold one down by an end and blow air from a hair dryer across it. Try this with both strips. Both strips should wave violently, but which one is the strip that twists?

Eeeeee eeeeee...

Wind-Swept!

The Tacoma Narrows Bridge was very long, but its deck was narrow, only 39 feet (12 m) across. Along the deck's sides were solid, flat pieces of steel, meant to stiffen the deck. But they weren't high enough for such a long and narrow bridge. All these factors made the Tacoma twist too easily.

As the wind blew, it hit the Tacoma's solid side. It had no place to go but over and under the bridge. Swirls of air were created on the other side, causing the bridge to vibrate. As the waves got bigger, the deck started twisting.

What happened to the Tacoma shocked engineers. They had ignored reports on why the Wheeling (see page 55) had collapsed. After the disaster, bridge engineers stopped making the plates along the sides of decks solid. Instead, new plates had openings to let wind go through.

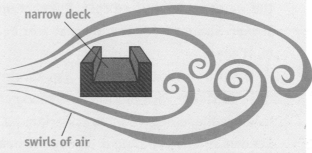

narrow deck

swirls of air

ANSWER: The narrow one twists, just as the narrow, flat deck twisted.

PEOPLE MAKE IT HAPPEN

Joseph Strauss

Golden Gate Bridge • San Francisco • 1937

The Poet and the Bridge

The mile-wide (1.6-km) inlet between the Pacific Ocean and California's San Francisco Bay is a beautiful site, but not an easy place to build a bridge. Strong tides sweep through four times a day and the water is choppy and cold. But that didn't stop **Joseph Strauss** from arguing that a bridge could be built there.

Strauss was a dreamer and a poet, but he also liked to tinker with machines. Although he didn't have a college degree in engineering, he did have his own bridge-building company. He beat out 11 other engineers and was chosen chief engineer on the project in 1930.

Despite accidents and storms, the tall steel towers went up, two thick cables were spun (see page 57), and the roadway was laid. Everyone who had said it couldn't be done, everyone who had hurled insults at Strauss, everyone who had predicted it would ruin the beauty of the site, now could only gaze in wonder at the slender orange ribbon hanging in the sky. *The Golden Gate Bridge* had become Strauss's greatest poem.

Flexing Your Brain

It's easy to get frustrated when things don't go according to plan. But to get the job done, it's important to be flexible, to be able to adapt to a new situation.

Take Joseph Strauss, for example. When his original plan for building the southern foundation on the Golden Gate didn't work, he tried something else. He turned a problem into a success. What he *didn't* do was to insist his first way was the only way.

Think about a situation you've been in lately, in which a different approach would have worked better. What kept you or others from changing? Stubbornness? Too much pride? Embarrassment about being wrong? Well, you know what? Being flexible enough to say, "This won't work," is a great benefit when you are a team player. Sometimes it is called "thinking on your feet."

Take The Challenge!

The Job:

You are asked to design a bridge that will cross a wide strip of water connecting one big lake to another.

The Site:

The lakes are in northern Michigan where the wind howls and ice is common in winter. The strip of water to be crossed is 5 miles (8 km) wide. The water is deep only in the middle. Bedrock there is 200 feet (61 m) under the surface of the water. The time is the early 1950s, so steel and reinforced concrete are available. And, oh yeah, you were on the team of engineers who investigated the Tacoma Narrows disaster (see page 64).

The Challenges:

There's that wind to worry about. Tacoma is still on your mind. And, of course, the distance to be spanned is incredibly long. Plus, there's the possibility that chunks of ice could knock down piers and crash into foundations.

Things to Consider:

Think about looking to the past for answers. Remember the lesson engineers learned about stabilizing a bridge in wind? Also, remember that the side spans and approaches of a bridge can be long or short. You'll need a way to protect the piers and foundations from ice, too.

This bridge-building job was real. All these problems were faced by American engineer David Steinman when he built the Mackinac [MAK-in-nak] *Bridge in the 1950s over the strait between two of the Great Lakes, Huron and Michigan. Steinman was even involved in investigating the Tacoma. After you solve the problems, read how Steinman did it on page 89.*

BRIDGES
on the Move

Usually we think of people, cars, and trains moving across bridges, but sometimes it's the bridge that does the moving. If you live near a canal or river, you may have seen a *drawbridge* at work. Or maybe you've seen a *vertical lift-bridge* over another waterway. These bridges, as well as the *swing* and *transporter*, are all bridges that move.

Once steel was on the scene, there was a perfect material for movable bridges, because steel is strong yet light enough to be easily moved. And new technology and production of engines and motors helped in the development and operation of moving bridges.

But if you counted all the bridges in the world (now *that* would be a fun job!), you wouldn't find many movable ones. Why? Although they are fascinating to watch, movable bridges are very expensive to build and need lots of maintenance.

Draw Up the Bridge!

Suddenly, your home is under attack by a band of enemies! What do you do? If you lived long ago in a medieval castle surrounded by a moat, you'd raise the wooden drawbridge and keep the bad guys out! Back then, drawbridges were usually kept in a lowered position (except in times of danger) to let people cross the moat. Today, drawbridges are kept in lowered position for cars and trucks to use. When tall ships come through, they're raised.

Materials:

↞ **Empty cereal box**
↢ **Scissors**
↧ **Hole punch**
↘ **String**

1. *Cut the top flaps off the box. Punch holes near the top corners of the back and front of the box.*

2. *Thread the string first through one of the back holes and, then, through the front hole on the same side.*

3. *Bring the string across the front and thread it through the front and back holes. Cut along each side of the front of the box.*

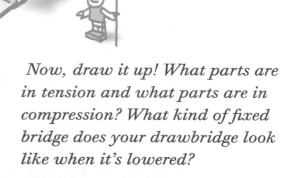

Now, draw it up! What parts are in tension and what parts are in compression? What kind of fixed bridge does your drawbridge look like when it's lowered?

The City of Moving Bridges

Bascule over the Chicago River

Driving around downtown Chicago, Illinois, you find yourself crossing over water again and again on a series of movable bridges. Chicago became the city of moving bridges during the 20th century.

For most of the century, the city had two "working rivers." The Chicago and the Calumet rivers were home to freighters and other large ships making their way from the ocean, across the Great Lakes, and down the rivers to deliver products to the city. As Chicago grew, the rivers interrupted traffic. A system of *bascules* (BAHSK-yools), or drawbridges, was designed. City officials wanted bridges that were level with the street and allowed both river and road traffic to go through.

Think About It

Making Up Your Mind

Every day we all make lots of decisions — from what kind of cereal to have for breakfast to whether to wear sneakers or sandals. And, some decisions are definitely bigger than others.

So, what is the process for decision making? It all depends. Some choices are instantaneous; you just know what you want to do. Others require careful thought, discussion, and some research. Then, perhaps you would use the process of elimination the way Chicago did, listing all the choices and carefully eliminating those that won't work. Next time you just can't decide, try it!

Chicago's Choices

Why choose a bascule? Well, let's think about the challenges the city faced: The rivers were very narrow, and there wasn't much space on the shore. Would any fixed bridge work?

- *Suspension bridges* need lots of land for their long approaches. Besides, they're meant to span long distances.
- *Arches* can only get tall enough to allow high-masted ships to pass underneath when the river is wide.
- A *simple beam bridge* wouldn't let ships pass through at all.

What's left? *Movable bridges*. But what kind would work best? Well, the city had an old swing bridge that created a traffic hazard in the water with its center pier. A vertical-lift bridge worked, but everyone thought it was ugly. So, the drawbridge it was!

⚙ HOW IT WORKS! ⚙

Drawbridges, or bascules, have been around since the days of castles and knights, when strong people pulled on thick ropes or chains to raise them. Nowadays, bascules have heavy weights on one end that equal the weight of the bridge. Electric motors push the weights down, causing the bridge to lift up.

The part of a bascule that goes up and down is called a *leaf*. To bridge wider gaps, there can be two leaves that meet in the middle and are locked in place when lowered.

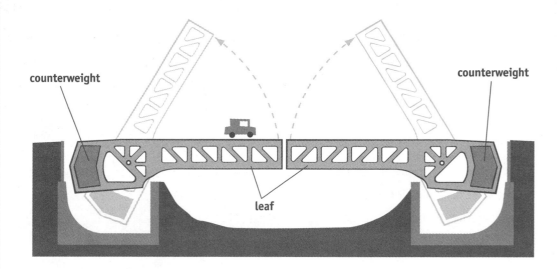

counterweight

counterweight

leaf

COUNTERBALANCED

The word bascule is French for "seesaw," which helps explain how modern bascules work. They're counterbalanced by weights, which make them work better than old castle drawbridges. See for yourself by tying a block to the string of your homemade drawbridge (see page 69) to help raise it.

Make a Double-Leaf Bascule

Now that you know how to make a single-leaf bascule (see page 69), try your hand at making a double-leaf bascule. Be sure to figure out a way to lock the leaves in place, but don't forget — they still have to move.

The Wonder Bridge

Tower Bridge • London, England • 1894

Road Trip

Watching movable bridges in action almost brings them to life! Check out locations of movable bridges near you or where you will be visiting on a vacation. Perhaps there's a swing bridge across a river or a bascule over a canal. Before you go, think of some questions to ask the bridge operator, and plan to park the car and watch for a while. Here are a few questions to get you started:

- Does the bridge work on a schedule, or does it go up and down on demand?
- What does the operator have to do to make the bridge move?
- How many boats pass through in a day?
- Are there any interesting stories about this bridge?

"Monstrous!" "Preposterous!" Those are the words Londoners once used to describe the *Tower Bridge*, an unusual drawbridge crossing the Thames River. The bridge, nicknamed "The Wonder Bridge," was completed in 1894. It used the power of water, called *hydraulic power*, made from steam engines to lift its leaves.

Because the Thames was wide where this bridge was to be built, a single- or double-leaf bascule wouldn't do. Yet a moving bridge was needed because of the sailing vessels that used the river. There were also pedestrians to think about. A double-leaf bascule between two towers, plus two side spans and a pedestrian walkway was the creative answer.

In the early days, sailors simply honked their horns with one long and three short blasts, and the bridge master would open the bridge. Horns were honking close to 6,000 times a year! Today, boat owners must notify the operator a day in advance. The number of bridge openings has gone way down to about 500 per year. It takes less than a minute to raise this "Wonder Bridge."

The Tower Bridge still stands; check it out at its Web site: http://www.southwark.gov.uk/tourism/attractions/tower_bridge/

Lift That Bridge!

Vertical-lift bridges have one section that moves up horizontally, allowing ships to pass under them. They're good for wide waterways. Unfortunately, many people think they look ugly because of all the machinery needed to make them work. Make this simple version yourself and discover its unique way of working.

Materials:

- Hole punch, scissors, and string
- 1 piece of thin cardboard (about the size of the boxes)
- 2 empty cereal boxes (the same size)
- A drinking straw, cut in half

1. *To prepare the bridge span, punch a hole in each corner of the cardboard.*

2. *To prepare the towers, cut the top flaps from each cereal box. Punch holes on the front and back of the boxes.*

3. *To assemble the bridge, arrange the string guide wires so the span can be raised evenly. Put string through one corner of the span and, then, through the bottom hole of one tower.*

4. *Bring the string up inside the tower and out a front hole on the same side. Tie the ends together tightly. Repeat for the other corner. Then, repeat for the other tower.*

continued

5. *Cut two pieces of string, each about 5 feet (1.5 m). Tie one piece around one hole in the span. Then, lace it through the second hole at the top of the tower and out through the hole in the back. Pull the string through half a straw.*

6. *Feed the string through the other hole in the back of the tower and out the front. Tie it off at the hole on the other side of the span. Tie it so the straw hangs level, about 2 inches (5 cm) down the tower. Repeat steps 5 and 6 for the other tower.*

7. *To make your bridge work, grasp the straws and gently pull down. Watch your bridge rise! Can you think of other ways to lift up your bridge? Try making pulleys from cardboard tubes and adding weights to the straws.*

BACK VIEW

TIED OFF UNDER HERE

YAY!

Jack! Are you playing with your food again?

A Double-Decker Bridge?

That's right! The *Willamette River Bridge* in Portland, Oregon is a so-called *dual vertical-lift bridge*. Trains zoom along the lower deck, while cars whiz by on the top.

Bridge It with a Swing

Yet another movable bridge is the swing bridge, *a steel cantilever that pivots on a huge drumlike support, usually placed in the middle of the movable span. Swing bridges can cross wider waterways than other movable bridges, and tall ships can pass by them easily, too, but they take up lots of room. Make one for yourself to see how they work.*

Materials:

← Thin cardboard
↙ Scissors
↓ Paper fastener
↘ Rectangular cake pan
→ Plastic container with a lid (an old margarine container works well)
↗ Rocks

1. *Cut a piece of thin cardboard for a span as long as the pan is wide. Push a paper fastener through its center and then through the lid.*

2. *Fill the container with rocks. Put the lid on and place it in the cake pan.*

3. *Fill the pan with water so that toy boats can float, but your bridge span doesn't get wet.*

4. *Cut out a cardboard road leading to your bridge. Build up the road so it's level with the sides of the pan. Now, swing your bridge and sail your toy boats by!*

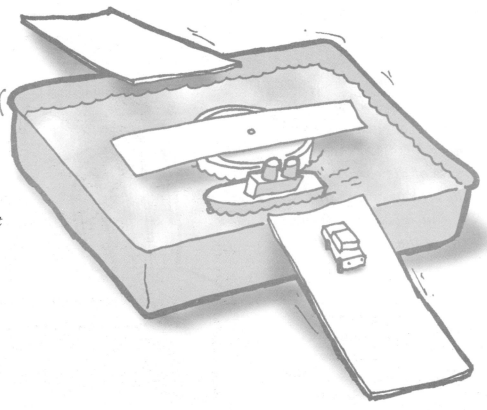

Build a Transporter Bridge

When something's obsolete, it means it's outdated and not used anymore. That's the case with transporter bridges. They're kind of fun, but they're not very practical. These movable bridges were used where there were lots of boats using the water and only a small number of people crossing it.

A transporter bridge is a platform hanging from a metal frame that carries cars and people. It's pulled back and forth from shore to shore by a system of cables.

Materials:
ⅩⅩⅩⅩⅩⅩⅩⅩⅩⅩⅩⅩ

← 2 open-backed chairs
↰ Hole punch, tape, scissors, and roll of string
↧ 5" x 7" (13 cm x 18 cm) piece of cardboard
↘ Two 5-inch (13-cm) drinking straws
→ Small, shallow box lid

1. Begin by spacing the chairs 3 to 4 feet (about 1 m) apart.

2. Punch holes in each corner of the cardboard and in the center of each edge of the longer sides. On the underside of the cardboard, tape the straws across the width, 1 inch (2.5 cm) from the ends of the cardboard.

3. Tie one end of a piece of string to one chair. Lace it through one straw and tie it tightly to the other chair. Repeat on other side.

Bottom

Guide line

4. *Tie another piece of string to one center hole, wrapping it around one chair. Bring the string across to the other chair and back again to tie off at the other center hole.*

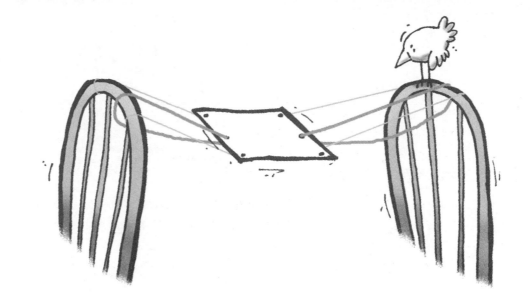

5. *Next, make the car ferry by cutting four pieces of string. Tape one end of each piece to the lid. Tape the other ends to the corner holes of the cardboard so that the lid is level with the seat when it hangs. The seats of the chairs are the roads.*

continued

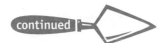

6. *Pull the center string to move the bridge back and forth. Add small cars to your ferry to find out how much load your bridge can carry. Make gates on your lid and drive your cars on board.*

Take The Challenge!

The Job:
Choose a movable bridge design for each of the following settings. (Each bridge can be a different type of movable bridge.)

The Sites:
1. A city with a system of narrow canals running through it. At one end, there's a marina where tall sailboats can dock and get repairs.

2. A wide river where trains need to cross twice a day. Boat traffic is heavy.

3. A wide stretch of water separating a resort area from an island with a wildlife sanctuary on it. No cars are allowed on the island, so the bridge is for pedestrians only. Pleasure boats and sailboats frequently travel up and down the channel.

The Challenges:
In this ideal situation, there are no limitations. You can spend as much as you want and use whatever materials you need.

Things to Consider:
A movable bridge is obviously needed at each site. But what's the best type for each setting? What are your options? As you sketch designs, think through all the advantages and disadvantages of each one, using the process of elimination to make your decision.

The Care & Feeding of BRIDGES

The foundations are laid. The cables are spun. The road is paved. The bridge is done, right? Guess again! Once a bridge is built, it's never really finished. Like you, it needs checkups to keep it in tip-top shape. Only with bridges, it's not doctors who do the checking — it's inspectors and engineers.

Think About It

Cost-Saving Care

The Golden Gate has a brigade of workers who inspect, repair, and paint the bridge. But many major bridges in North America, including those in major cities, don't have regular maintenance crews assigned to them. Without continual maintenance, simple problems become major headaches. Bridges are sometimes in such disrepair, they have to be completely redone. Imagine how much that costs!

Yet, according to one estimate, for every dollar spent on bridge maintenance, three dollars are saved in future repairs. So what do you think the problem is? Why aren't bridges being cared for, when maintenance is less costly than complete overhauls?

Can You Believe It?

The U.S. Navy wanted the Golden Gate to be painted black with yellow stripes to make it easier to spot. Instead of the beauty that graces the bay, the bridge might have looked like a giant bee buzzing around!

Rusting Steel

To keep the Golden Gate its beautiful reddish color (called International Orange), a team of painters is on the bridge every day. That's because the Golden Gate is made of steel, and steel rusts. You can see the effects of rust for yourself right in your own kitchen!

Gather three small plastic containers and three small pieces of steel wool. Put one piece into each container. With a grown-up's help, bring some water to a boil for a minute or two. Cool. Pour the water into one of the containers, completely covering the steel wool. In the second container, cover the steel wool with water from the kitchen faucet. Don't add any water to the third container.

Check the containers in a few hours or the next day. Meanwhile, keep in mind that for steel to rust, it must be exposed to water and oxygen. Oxygen is found in air and water. Boiling removes oxygen from the water. Now that you know these facts, what will you expect to see?

Leave the experiment for a week. So why is the Golden Gate tended by painters every day?

CONQUERING RUST

Paint is a good weapon to fight rust on the steel you can see on towers and trusses, but what about the steel you can't see, like the rods used inside reinforced concrete? We think of concrete as being solid because it can take a lot of compression. But it's actually *porous*, which means it has lots of little holes in it. Water that seeps into the holes rusts the steel in places paintbrushes can't reach.

To prevent rusting, engineers now use steel rods that have a special coating. These coated reinforcing bars, or *rebar*, last a long time. They are also beginning to use rods made out of materials that don't rust, like plastic and carbon. Since these newer rods have only been used a short time, engineers don't know how long they will last.

I should have brought a bigger brush.

TIRED BRIDGES

You know the feeling. You're so tired you can barely brush your teeth or put on your pj's. You fall into bed, and your eyes are closed before your head hits the pillow! Would you believe that bridges get tired, or *fatigued*, too? Each day, bridges are being pushed and pulled, pulled and pushed, right down to the smallest nuts and bolts. As tension and compression forces are applied and removed over and over again, materials gradually get weaker.

Try This! Bend a paper clip back and forth until it breaks. How many bends does it take? Changes in temperature have the same effect. They cause metal to break down.

Tired Old Muscles

Feel what fatigue is all about by holding a hardcover book in one hand. Now, lift the book up and down by bending and straightening your elbow all the way. How many times can you lift the book before one minute is up?

Now, wait a moment and repeat, using the same arm. Record. Wait another minute and do it again. How does your arm feel? When you think about the thousands of cars that travel over bridges each day, it's no wonder they get fatigued!

Soap Saves the Day

While it's true that concrete suffers from fatigue, too, more of its problems come from things that attack it from the inside. Because concrete is porous, water can leak into those holes, creating lots of problems, especially when it freezes. Ice takes up more room and pushes outward on the concrete, causing it to crumble.

Try This! Fill a small plastic container with water all the way to the top. Put the lid on and place it in the freezer. After it's frozen, check what happened.

Help is on the way with a new detergent made from pinetree sap. It makes lots of bubbles as it's mixed into concrete. When ice forms, it pops the bubbles and takes up their space. There's room for the ice, so it puts less pressure on the concrete.

SALT ATTACK!

Concrete's number one enemy isn't water — it's salt. These days we shake salt on our highways as though they were french fries! Salt prevents ice from building up on roads, making them safer in the winter. But that salt gets into the same little holes that water does. The salt attacks the steel rods inside the reinforced concrete, causing them to corrode. That's another reason why engineers now use *coated* rebar to help prevent corrosion. It helps, but salt still manages to do plenty of damage.

Great Idea!

Soap from sap? Detergent in cement? Ice popping bubbles? It all makes perfect sense — once someone thought of it! It's called "thinking outside the box." That means using what you know in unusual places.

We all know that soap makes bubbles, but who ever thought of using that bit of information to solve the problem of crumbling concrete in winter? Next time you come face-to-face with a problem, think beyond the usual and you may come up with the perfect solution!

CHECKING A BRIDGE'S HEARTBEAT

Of course, bridges don't really have heartbeats. But engineers have a new tool that's like a stethoscope, used to "listen" to what's going on inside a concrete structure.

A small steel ball swings out and taps the concrete, creating vibrations that go through the concrete and then echo back. A laptop computer records the echoes. If the vibrations travel through cracks or crevices, the echoes look different. A printout shows any weak spots and cracks, much as an X-ray would show if you had a broken bone.

Making Good Bridges Better

Sixty seconds. That's how long it would take for a major earthquake to destroy the historic Golden Gate Bridge. But don't worry; no one's sitting idly by waiting for that to happen. Early in the 1990s, seismic engineers (experts in understanding how earthquakes affect structures) discovered that, although the Golden Gate had lived through several large earthquakes, if one hit closer, the bridge might not survive.

So a retrofit was begun to strengthen parts of the bridge and stabilize it so there is less bridge movement when the ground shakes. It's a big job that's expected to cost $175 million. Compared with the cost of building a new, stronger bridge — $1.4 billion — that's a bargain!

Smart Concrete?

Concrete is getting smarter every day. How's that? Scientists can now insert sensors (strings thinner than a strand of hair) into concrete. Computers are hooked up to analyze information from the sensors so problems can be fixed.

Recently, steel has smartened up, too. Engineers from the University of Vermont have placed sensors on the steel trusses of the *Winooski River Bridge* to check for cracks and decay.

Inspect Your Home

To help prevent failures, bridges have to be kept in good shape. The same is true for all structures, including our homes. But repairing and replacing parts in a building cost money and take time.

Ask your parents or building superintendent what is involved in the care and repair of your home. Then, make a calendar showing what jobs are done at what time of the year.

* *The original Point Pleasant Bridge was nicknamed "Silver Bridge" because of its color. Today, there are two cantilever bridges at the same site, called* Silver Memorial 1 *and* Silver Memorial 2.

A Case of Bridge Fatigue

LEARNING FROM **DISASTERS!**

On a cold December evening in 1967, hundreds of Christmas shoppers and commuters were hurrying home when the suspension bridge they were traveling on suddenly collapsed. Forty-six people died when the *Point Pleasant Bridge** between Ohio and West Virginia fell into the frigid Ohio River.

Investigators wanted to know what happened so, working in a large field, they put the bridge back together. After three years, the scientists had their answer. In the summer, heat made the metal in the bridge *expand* (get bigger), while cold made it *contract* (get smaller) in the winter. Forty years of expanding and contracting weakened one piece of metal so much it got fatigued. This eventually made the whole bridge break down. Following this bridge's failure, the United States began a program of regular bridge inspections and repair.

Learn the Lingo

After New York's *Schoharie Creek Thruway Bridge* collapsed in 1987, divers discovered that *scour* was the culprit. Scour happens when sand and soil are washed away by moving water, much like when you stand on the beach after a wave recedes, and your heels sink because the sand behind your feet has washed away. Scour happens naturally around a bridge's piers, so it's important for sand to be replaced before scour gets dangerously deep.

Cornish–Windsor Covered Bridge

Take The Challenge!

Many of the bridges being restored in the United States today are covered bridges (see page 43), a link to the country's history and simpler times.

The Job:

Decide whether to restore the *Cornish–Windsor Covered Bridge* or replace it with a concrete beam bridge.

The Site:

Crossing the Connecticut River, the bridge joins Cornish, New Hampshire, with Windsor, Vermont. It's located in a scenic wooded area that people have enjoyed for years. Built in 1866, it had to be closed for safety reasons. The year is 1987.

The Challenges:

Restoration may cost as much as $5 million. Although a concrete beam bridge may cost more than that, a covered bridge is more susceptible to fire damage and wood rot. The type of wood used in the bridge deck and roof is harder to come by these days, making it difficult and expensive to restore the bridge to its original design.

Things to Consider:

The bridge is located in New England, one of many regions that takes pride in its heritage and beautiful landscape. The Cornish–Windsor is listed on the National Register of Historic Places. It's also the longest two-lane covered bridge in North America. Businesses on both sides of the river have suffered since the bridge has been closed.

Bridges to the Future

"Must we admit that because a thing
has never been done it can never be?"

— James Eads
BUILDER & DESIGNER OF BRIDGE ACROSS THE MISSISSIPPI RIVER

Great bridge builders of the past, like John Roebling (see page 55) and Joseph Strauss (see page 66), were bold and imaginative. They dared to dream of doing things that had not been done before.

There are still dreamers today, and who knows, maybe you will be one in the future! Perhaps you imagine designing or engineering a majestic bridge, or maybe you'll invent a new material or technique. Yes, it certainly could be you. Are you daring enough to look to the future and see what it holds?

PEOPLE MAKE IT HAPPEN

T.Y. Lin

Today's Dreamer

Ten thousand feet (3,048 m)! Given today's materials and know-how, that's the longest a single bridge span can be, say many engineers. Longer than that, the materials would give out.

But **T.Y. Lin**, an American engineer, says longer is possible. He dreams of connecting continents, not across oceans, but where the land almost touches.

Lin has already come up with an award-winning design for a bridge across the Strait of Gibraltar, the body of water between Spain in Europe and Morocco in Africa. He also dreams of bringing together Asia and North America across the Bering Strait; his *Intercontinental Peace Bridge*, as Lin calls it, would cross the unbelievable distance of 55 miles (87 km).

Lin believes today's high-strength steel invented to build Japan's *Akashi Kaikyo*, the longest suspension bridge ever built, will be strong enough for his long spans. Other engineers suggest that new, lighter materials made with plastic and other artificial materials would be better. Still, the mere fact this is being debated indicates that Lin's big thinking is taking hold as a possibility.

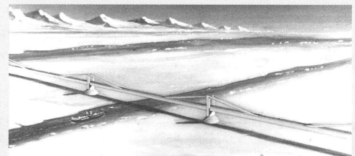

Lin's concept for the Intercontinental Peace Bridge • Bering Strait

SPANNING THE STRAITS

Lin's concept for Strait of Gibraltar crossing • Europe to Africa

T.Y. Lin's design for the Strait of Gibraltar includes two main spans, each over 15,000 feet (4,572 m) in length. So how does Lin plan to do this? By combining features from suspension and cable-stayed bridges to create a new design.

A suspension bridge can be compared to a person wearing suspenders that hold up trousers from the shoulders — just like the hangers hold up a bridge deck from its cables. In a cable-stayed design, the deck hangs directly from the cables like pants from a belt. When you combine hangers and cable-stays, it's like wearing both suspenders and a belt. It's a surefire way to keep your pants — oops, the deck — up!

star pattern

harp pattern

radiating pattern

⚙ HOW IT WORKS! ⚙

In a cable-stayed bridge, sections of the deck hang by cables attached to towers, called *pylons*. The weight of the deck and its traffic pulls on the cables, which then pull on the pylons. The pylons pass the force down to the foundations. Cable-stayed bridges can't be as long as suspension bridges, but they are cheaper to build.

Build a Cable-Stayed Bridge

Lin is looking into the future by combining features of the suspension bridge and the cable-stayed bridge. That plus new materials could move bridge-building forward.

Design and build your own cable-stayed bridge. Choose one of the three traditional cable patterns, or look to the future by inventing your own. You might want to make two bridges with different patterns and compare their strength's under a load.

You'll need pieces of stiff cardboard for the deck, tape to connect deck pieces, string for the cables, and scissors. You can use chairs for the pylons, but don't rest any part of the deck directly on the chair. That would be cheating! Or, you can stick two poles in the ground outside. For piers under the side spans, you can use cardboard rolls from paper towels. Or, try using new materials that accomplish your design goals.

Old Materials Made New

Scientists are researching new materials to build stronger bridges and solve problems older materials have. *Composites* are materials that have two or more ingredients, kind of like ice cream that has nuts and chocolate chips in it. They're mixed together to make something that's stronger, lighter, lasts longer, or is more flexible. Plastic can have threads of glass, called fibers, added. Concrete can be mixed with fibers made of steel, plastic, glass, or carbon. There's even something new called "cement lite." It's so light and bendable that it can even be used to make business cards.

So far, composites have only been used in real structures in a very limited way. More testing is needed to see if the new stuff is better than the old or if it just gives engineers more materials to choose from. But as long as people are thinking in terms of better materials, change will happen.

SPANNING TIME

Imagine the bridge builders of the Middle Ages sitting around, toying with quill pen and parchment, sketching designs to help transport people and horses from here to there. Think of the Romans figuring out the mathematical calculations for their arches. Why, even a few decades ago, it took engineers several months to solve those same equations. These days, computers have made things much easier and faster!

Months of solving equations and figuring load capacity have been reduced to days with the help of super-accurate Computer Aided Design and Drafting (CADD) programs. Computers do something else that makes bridge design easier — they can show what a bridge would look like in 3-D.

By moving an image up and down and all around, you can see how it looks from all angles.

Computers are also used to see how storms and earthquakes affect bridge designs. A drawing is put on the screen and tortured with gale-force winds and violent shaking forces, telling engineers if a bridge would survive. Changes can then be made to make the bridge stronger. With computers, engineers can feel confident that the bridges they're building are the sturdiest and safest possible.

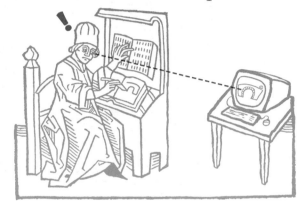

SMALL STEPS AND BOLD CONCEPTS

"The great advances of the human race have been won by those who showed the courage to go beyond the charted course."

–David Steinman

BUILDER OF THE MACKINAC BRIDGE IN MICHIGAN

An idea can be a simple step forward. Other times it's an inspiration that stretches imaginations to create bold new concepts. The results from each? A brand-new design. An awesome new material. A better way of doing things.

Remember the challenge on page 67? **David Steinman** actually faced these challenges. He solved the distance problem by combining a long suspended span with extra-long side spans. He

added a long approach on either side of the anchors to reach the shores. These approaches are sturdy truss-beam bridges.

He braced the bridge with very deep trusses under the roadway to make it rigid. He left space in between and put vents in the deck to let wind pass through to keep it from vibrating.

To build very strong foundations, Steinman used huge caissons to reach the bedrock. Then, stones were dumped into the caissons and cement and sand were pumped in on top. Steel towers provided all the support the cables needed.

Did your ideas come close to what Steinman did? Did you "think outside the box" to solve your site consideration?

Take The Challenge!

If you could build the bridge of your dreams anywhere in the world, where would it be? Perhaps there's an island off the coast of a continent, or two countries that you think should be connected. Use a map or globe if you need some help finding such a place. Once you've picked your site, get some paper and colored pencils, and start drawing.

What type of bridge will you design? A super-long suspension? A combination design like T.Y. Lin's? Or maybe you have a dream all your own? Whatever you come up with, think about the problems your site presents. How will you solve them? Think about the materials you'll need. Can parts of your bridge be made out of composites, or are you going to rely on trusty steel and concrete?

Now, add some color. Something wild like stripes? Or do you prefer your bridge to blend with its natural surroundings?

Then, build a model of your bridge. Gather materials that you used for the other bridges you've built, like Popsicle sticks, string, and cardboard, or find something new. Make your dream for the future come true!

List of Bridges by State

The following is a list of the bridges mentioned in this book (marked with *), some of the longest bridges, and well-known bridges of different types in the United States, Canada, and around the world. Many bridges are famous for reasons other than length, of course. The best way to find out about bridges you might visit is to contact your town's or city's Highway Department to find out about the bridges near where you live or visit.

IN THE UNITED STATES

Alabama
I-65 Mobile River Bridge (arch)
Cochrane Bridge (cable-stayed)

Alaska
Douglas Bridge (beam)
Tanana River Bridge (truss)

Arizona
Roosevelt Lake (arch)
Glen Canyon Bridge (arch)

Arkansas
Rte. 49 Helena Bridge (cantilever)

California
*Golden Gate Bridge (suspension), pages 66, 83
Transbay Bridge (cantilever, suspension, beam)
San Diego-Coronado Bridge (beam)
Bridgeport Covered Bridge (covered)
Carquinez Strait Bridge (cantilever)
Martinez Bridge (movable)

Colorado
Royal Gorge Bridge (suspension)

Connecticut
Gold Star Memorial Bridge (truss)
Rt. 82 Connecticut River Bridge (movable)

Delaware
Summit Bridge (truss)
Delaware Memorial Bridge (suspension)
Chesapeake and Delaware Canal Bridge (cable-stayed)
Pennsylvania Railroad Bridge (movable)

Florida
Acosta Bridge (beam)
John E. Matthews Bridge (truss)
Isaiah D. Hart Bridge (cantilever)
Dames Point Bridge (cable-stayed)
Sunshine Skyway Bridge (cable-stayed)
Main Street Bridge (movable)

Georgia
Talmadge Memorial Bridge (cable-stayed)

Idaho
Perrine Bridge (arch)
Grandad Bridge (truss)
Dent Bridge (suspension)

Illinois
I-57 Bridge (arch)
Chester Bridge (truss)
Bayview Bridge (cable-stayed)
Michigan Avenue Bridge (movable)

Illinois-Kentucky
Earl C. Clement Bridge (truss)
Cairo Bridge (cantilever)

Illinois-Missouri
MacArthur Bridge (truss)

Indiana
I-64 Sherman Minton Bridge (arch)
Matthew E. Welsh Bridge (truss)

Indiana-Kentucky
Lincoln Trail Bridge (arch)
US 31 Bridge (truss)

Iowa
Dubuque Bridge (truss)
Burlington Bridge (cable-stayed)
Fort Madison Bridge (movable)

Kansas-Missouri
A-S-B Fratt Bridge (movable)

Kentucky
13th Street Bridge (truss)
Carl Perkins Bridge (cantilever)
Simon Kenton Memorial Bridge (suspension)

Kentucky-Ohio
Brent Spence Bridge (cantilever)

Louisiana
Lake Pontchartrain Bridge 1 & 2 (beam)
Greater New Orleans Bridge 1 & 2 (cantilever)
Hale Boggs Memorial Bridge (cable-stayed)
East Pearl River Bridge (movable)

Maine
Piscataqua River Bridge (truss)
Patapsco River Bridge (cantilever)
Deer Isle Bridge (suspension)

Maryland
Francis Scott Key Bridge (truss)
William Preston Lane Memorial Bridge 2 (suspension)

Massachusetts
Charles Braga Memorial Bridge (truss)
Cape Cod Canal Bridge (movable)

Michigan
*Mackinac Bridge (suspension), pages 67, 89
Blue Water Bridge (cantilever)

Minnesota
Lake Street Bridge (arch)
Blatnik Bridge (truss)
Duluth Bridge (movable)

Mississippi
Mississippi River Bridge (cantilever)

Missouri
*Eads Bridge (arch), page 86
Poplar Street Bridge (beam)
Cape Girardeau Bridge (truss)
Martin Luther King Bridge (cantilever)
A-S-B Fratt Bridge (movable)

Missouri-Tennessee
Caruthersville Bridge (cantilever)

Montana
Lake Koocanusa Bridge (truss)

New Hampshire-Vermont
*Cornish–Windsor Covered Bridge (covered), page 85

New Jersey
*New Jersey Turnpike (beam), page 37
Pulaski Skyway Bridge (truss)
Delair Bridge (movable)

New Mexico
Rio Grande Gorge Bridge (truss)

New York
*Brooklyn Bridge (suspension), pages 56-59
*Erie Canal Bridge (first iron bridge), page 44
*Schoharie Creek Thruway Bridge (beam), page 85
Hell Gate Bridge (arch)
Kingston-Rhinecliff Bridge (truss)
Marine Parkway Bridge (movable)
Tappan Zee Bridge (cantilever)
Verrazano-Narrows Bridge (suspension)
*Whirlpool Rapids Bridge (arch), page 35

New York-New Jersey
*George Washington Bridge (suspension), page 63
Bayonne (Kill Van Kull) Bridge (arch)
Arthur Kill Bridge (movable)

North Carolina
Cape Fear Memorial Bridge (movable)

Ohio
Cincinnati Railroad Bridge (truss)
Norfolk Southern Railroad Bridge (cantilever)
Lorain Bridge (movable)

Oregon
*Willamette River Bridge (movable), page 74
Fremont Bridge (arch)
McCullough Bridge (cantilever)
St. Johns Bridge (suspension)

Pennsylvania
Betsy Ross Bridge (truss)
Commodore Barry Bridge (cantilever)
Rochester-Monaca Bridge (truss)
Walt Whitman Bridge (suspension)
West End Bridge (arch)

Pennsylvania-New York
Roebling Bridge (Delaware Aqueduct)
(oldest wire suspension)

Rhode Island
*Newport Bridge (suspension), page 52
Jamestown Bridge (truss)
Jamestown-Verrazano Bridge (cantilever)

South Carolina
Mark Clark Expressway Bridge (truss)
Grace Memorial Bridge (cantilever)

South Dakota
Lake Oahe Bridges 1 & 2 (truss)

Tennessee
*Natchez Trace Parkway Arches (arch), page 31
US-64 Bridge (beam)
Memphis Bridge (cantilever)
SR-8 Tennessee River Bridge (movable)

Texas
Port Arthur-Orange Bridge (truss)
Houston Ship Channel Bridge (cable-stayed)
Corpus Christi Harbor Bridge (movable)

Utah
*Rainbow Bridge (natural arch), page 24

Vermont
*Winooski River Bridge (beam), page 83

Virginia
Chesapeake Bay Bridge (beam)
James River Bridge (cable-stayed)
US-17 York River Bridge (movable)

Washington
*Tacoma Narrows Bridge (suspension, rebuilt), pages 64-65
Selah Creek Twin Bridges (arch)
Hoffstadt Creek Bridge (truss)
Washington Memorial Bridge (cantilever)
Pasco-Kennewick (cable-stayed)
Evergreen Point Bridge (movable)

Washington-Oregon
Astoria Bridge (truss)
Lewis and Clark Bridge (cantilever)

Washington, D.C.
Douglass Memorial Bridge (movable)

West Virginia
*New River Gorge Bridge (arch), page 35
*Wheeling Bridge (suspension, rebuilt), page 55
Glade Creek Bridge (truss)
Ravenswood Bridge (cantilever)
*Harpers Ferry Bridge (beam, rebuilt), page 44

West Virginia-Ohio
*Silver Memorial Bridges 1 & 2 (cantilever), 84
Saint Marys Bridge (cantilever)
Veterans Memorial Bridge (cable-stayed)

Wisconsin
Mississippi River Bridge (beam)

BETWEEN UNITED STATES AND CANADA

Michigan-Ontario
Ambassador International Bridge (suspension)

New York-Ontario
*Niagara Bridge (original suspension replaced with steel arch bridge), page 55
Lewiston-Queenston Bridge (arch)
Seaway-Skyway Bridge (suspension)

IN CANADA

British Columbia
Port Mann Bridge (arch)
Lion's Gate Bridge (suspension)
Alex Fraser Bridge (cable-stayed)
Second Narrows Bridge (movable)

New Brunswick
Burton Bridge (beam)

New Brunswick-Quebec
Campbellton-Cross Point Bridge (cantilever)

Nova Scotia
Shubenacadie River Bridge (beam)
MacDonald Bridge (suspension)

Ontario
McDonald-Cartier Bridge (beam)
Burlington Bridge (movable)

Prince Edward Island-New Brunswick
*Confederation Bridge (beam), pages 50-51

Quebec
*Quebec Bridge (cantilever, rebuilt), page 49
Trois Rivieres Bridge (arch)
Champlain Bridge (truss)
Jacques Cartier Bridge (cantilever)
Pierre Laporte Bridge (suspension)
Papineau-Leblanc Bridge (cable-stayed)

INTERNATIONAL

Australia
Sydney Harbor Bridge (arch)

Brazil
Amizade Bridge (arch)
Costa e Silva Bridge (longest steel beam in world)

China
*Anji Bridge (arch), page 32,34
Wanxiang Bridge (longest concrete arch in world)
Jiangrin Bridge (suspension)
Tsing Ma Bridge (suspension)
Qingzhou Minjiang Bridge (cable-stayed)

Denmark
East Bridge Great Belt Fixed Link (suspension)

France
Pont Neuf (arch)
Pont d'Avignon (arch)
Tancarville Bridge (suspension)
Pont du Normandie (cable-stayed)

Germany
Duisberg-Rheinhausen Bridge (arch)
Rhine Bridge (suspension)
Severin Bridge (cable-stayed)

Italy
Ponte Vecchio (arch)
Rialto Bridge (arch)

Japan
*Akashi Kaikyo Bridge
(longest suspension in world), page 87
Nanko Bridge (cantilever)
Tatara Bridge (longest cable-stayed in world)

The Netherlands
Eramus Bridge (cable-stayed)

Norway
Stolmasundet Bridge (longest concrete beam in world)
Oskoy Island Bridge (suspension)
Skarnsundet Bridge (cable-stayed)

Spain
Lusitania (arch & beam)
Carlos Fernandez Casado Bridge (cable-stayed)

Sweden
Höga Kusten Bridge (suspension)
Sandö Bridge (arch)

United Kingdom
*London Bridge (arch), pages 38, 39
*Forth Bridge (cantilever), page 47
*Tay Bridge (beam, rebuilt), page 48
*Tower Bridge (movable), page 72
Runcorn-Widnes Bridge (arch)
Humber Bridge (suspension)
Menai Suspension Bridge (suspension)
Severn Bridge II (cable-stayed)

Index

Note: Page numbers in bold indicate photographs.

More Good Books from Williamson Publishing

KALEIDOSCOPE KIDS™ Books

Where Learning Meets Life
96 pages, two-color, fully
illustrated, 10 x 10,
$10.95, ages 6-12

Children's Book Council Notable Book
American Bookseller Pick of the Lists
Dr. Toy 10 Best Educational Products
PYRAMIDS!
**50 Hands-On Activities to Experience
Ancient Egypt**
by Avery Hart & Paul Mantell

Children's Book Council Notable Book
Parent's Guide Children's Media Award
American Bookseller Pick of the Lists
KNIGHTS & CASTLES
**50 Hands-On Activities to Experience
the Middle Ages**
by Avery Hart & Paul Mantell

ANCIENT GREECE!
**40 Hands-On Activities to Experience
this Wondrous Age**
by Avery Hart & Paul Mantell

American Bookseller Pick of the Lists
MEXICO!
**40 Activities to Experience Mexico Past
and Present**
by Susan Milord

THE BEAST IN YOU!
Activities & Questions to Explore Evolution
by Marc McCutcheon

GEOLOGY ROCKS!
50 Hands-on Activities to Explore the Earth
by Cindy Blobaum

Visit our Web site:
http://www.williamsonbooks.com
Or call 800-234-8791 for catalog.

To order:

Williamson Books are available from your favorite bookseller,
or directly from Williamson Publishing.

Toll-free phone orders: 1-800-234-8791
Visa or MasterCard accepted.

Or send to:

Williamson Publishing
P.O. Box 185, Charlotte, Vermont 05445

E-mail orders with credit cards: **order@williamsonbooks.com**
Catalog request: mail, phone, or e-mail

Postage is **$3.20** for first book and **$.50** for each additional book.
Fully guaranteed.

Kaleidoscope Kids™ is a trademark of Williamson Publishing.